Unwin Education Books: 34
THE COUNTESTHORPE EXPERIENCE

Unwin Education Books

Series Editor: Ivor Morrish, BD, BA, Dip.Ed (London), BA (Bristol)

Unwin Education Books: 34
Series Editor: Ivor Morrish

The Countesthorpe Experience

The First Five Years

Editor

JOHN WATTS
Principal, Countesthorpe College

London
GEORGE ALLEN & UNWIN LTD
RUSKIN HOUSE   MUSEUM STREET

Printed in Great Britain by
Biddles Ltd, Guildford, Surrey

This book is dedicated
to
Tim McMullen

Acknowledgements

Thanks and acknowledgements are due to the following who have kindly allowed use of their material:

Professor G. H. Bantock

The Editor, *Forum for the Discussion of New Trends in Education*

IMTEC (International Management Training for Educational Change)

The Editor, *Leicester Mercury* (front page 3 April 1973)

Maurice Temple Smith Ltd (*New Movements in the Study and Teaching of Chemistry*)

Routledge & Kegan Paul Ltd (from *The Role of the Head* edited by R. S. Peters)

The Schools Council and London University Institute of Education Joint Project Writing Across the Curriculum 11–13 Years and Ward Lock Educational (*Keeping Options Open*)

Times Newspapers Limited (two articles by Virginia Makins)

Contents

Introduction

It is not often that a group of teachers are called together to work out agreed aims and agreed operational procedures, to announce them and then start putting them into practice. Yet this is what Tim McMullen caused to happen in 1970 at Countesthorpe. The agreement produced a commitment and determination without which survival of the problematic opening years would have been impossible. On the other hand, although that announcement of intent caused widespread interest and excitement, it also produced anxiety and hostility. The early publicity drew both support and attack. During the early troubles we had to live on faith. By 1974, after our first wave of students had moved on to employment or higher education, we breathed again and felt we were no longer talking about what was going to happen but what was already happening. There was achievement now as well as aspiration.

At that point, a book became inevitable. We have had a steady bombardment of requests for information, visits, and invitations to talk at home and abroad. We have met these as best we can, but now some reasonably full and readable record is essential. At one point we had hoped to commission one writer to study our work and archives in order to report. But on considering what has already been written about us or generated from our own ranks, it was clear that with a certain amount of bridging, a book could be constructed from existing material.

We have attempted to restate our aims, to record the outlines of our history, to chart the philosophical currents through which we navigate, to place ourselves in a wider context of educational development, to indicate the political complexities of such a major innovation and, most difficult of all, to convey some impression of what it feels like here to be a student, a teacher, a parent or other member of the local community.

The book is therefore a dossier of case material. A framework has been devised to provide the reader with logical groupings and a sequence, even to provide an opportunity to pick and choose. But no attempt has been made to rewrite the varied component parts in one uniform style. There are also, inevitably, overlaps here and there. Indeed, it is hoped that overlap from differing standpoints may provide a stereoscopic effect. The short introductory passages are intended to identify those standpoints by saying just enough of the contributors and the circumstances under which each of these documents appeared.

The reader who wants a competent summary of it all by a reputable educational journalist will find it in Virginia Makins's contribution; Professor Brian Simon's opening article sets us in the line of development of public-maintained schooling, while the three concluding articles provide a view of our significance to others in Britain and overseas. Those interested in the philosophical question of what Education is may find stimulation from Michael Armstrong and Mike Minchin's articles, and possibly be illuminated as to how educationalists try to reconcile viewpoints but finally may agree to differ, by following the exchange of letters between Armstrong and Professor Bantock. Anyone looking for an immediate introduction to the atmosphere of working here could not do better than turn at once to the articles by Dave Claiden, Jeff Shapland and the students in Part III, and the middle section of 'Schools Within Schools'.

It is our hope that the Countesthorpe experience may now be shared more widely. This will have been worth doing if more school students, teachers and parents can see that a change is not always something that happens *to* us, but something we do, something we may to a greater extent choose to bring about.

J.W.

COUNTESTHORPE COLLEGE

The College consists of a comprehensive upper school for all boys and girls aged 14–16 within its catchment area, and beyond the age of compulsory attendance it offers the facilities needed by those in full-time non-vocational education and by those of any age who want part-time provision for recreational and academic activities. It is built to accommodate 1,400 students: at present there are some 900 full-time students and a thousand or so members of the locality who use it for part-time activities.

PART I
PERSPECTIVES

1

Countesthorpe in the Context of Comprehensive Development

BRIAN SIMON

BRIAN SIMON is Professor of Education at the University of Leicester School of Education. He is probably the most highly reputed chronicler and advocate of comprehensive schooling, author of The Common Secondary School, Studies in the History of Education *(3 vols),* Half Way There *(with Caroline Benn), and editor of* Forum for the Discussion of New Trends in Education. *Professor Simon is governing body of Countesthorpe College and has written this article chairman of the History of Education Society. He is a member of the specially as an opening for this book.*

Countesthorpe is an unusual school. Whether it is the prototype of the school of the future remains to be seen. But certainly it fuses together several new trends in English education and in that sense it is, perhaps, unique. While controversies have raged around – more particularly in the popular press and other media – staff and students have kept their heads, quietly and consistently pursuing their original objectives in a common accord, developing these and modifying their approach in the light of experience and consistent, intensive discussion. This has been impressive and bodes well for the future.

Since its foundation five years ago I have been a privileged observer and, to a minor extent, a participant. The first principal (Tim McMullen) invited me early on to act as one of his two nominees on the governing body and, when possible, I have consistently attended its meetings. But, more important, Countesthorpe is one of a number of local schools which offer school experience on a generous scale to students preparing to teach. The School of Education at the University of Leicester has taken full advantage of this, and for each of the five years of the school's existence up to as many as twenty postgraduate students each year have undertaken some of their teaching practice at Countesthorpe. There can be no doubt whatever as to the attitude of the great bulk of these students. They are fascinated by the school, by the enthusiasm and professional expertise of the staff they work with (who act as teacher–tutors), and by the whole approach and ambience of the place.

This connection has enabled me to keep in touch with developments at second-hand, and to estima'e the impression made by the school through the eyes (and experience) of young graduates preparing to teach. But in addition, a group of a dozen students under my aegis (and that of Deanne Boydell) carried through a detailed observational study of one year-group in 1971, which involved systematic observation of individual 14-year-old students – at weekly intervals over a full term at a formative stage in the school's development.* Finally, as a result of the close connection that has been built up between the university and school, many ex-students from the university's postgraduate certificate of education course are now teaching at Countesthorpe.

Having been closely concerned with the movement to comprehensive education for many years, I was particularly interested in the foundation of Countesthorpe, concentrating, as it did, in one institution a number of traditions already inherent in the comprehensive movement generally. While the College itself was established five years after the Labour Government's original Circular 10/65 (July 1965) which declared comprehensive education to be national policy, the county of Leicestershire had already established its first comprehensive schools, on the two-tier system (with a break at 14), in 1957 – and by 1969 had extended this system to cover the entire county (as it then was). In that year the selection examination at 11 was finally abolished. But of course the comprehensive school movement as a whole has a longer history than this, the first such schools having been established in the late 1940s. By the time Countesthorpe was founded there were over a thousand schools officially designated as comprehensive in Britain. In the process of their evolution, new tendencies and traditions emerged, based directly on the experience both of teachers and of local authorities who grappled with the new problems, and exploited the new opportunities, emerging in these schools of a new type. Many of these were embodied from the start in the thinking and practice of Countesthorpe.

What are these new developments? First, comprehensive schools are non-selective schools, taking in all the children in the locality; from the start such schools have been conceived as neighbourhood schools, usually with a defined catchment area – and so in a position to establish close links with the locality. Such is the position at Countesthorpe, which draws its students from an area south of Leicester. But, in line with the LEA's clear policy, Countesthorpe was originally designed as a community college, a focus of youth and adult educational and recreational activities as well as a school. This concept, which derives originally from Henry Morris's pioneer work in

---

* Ann Riley and Kathy Stamatakis, 'Countesthorpe College, an Observant Study', *Forum*, Vol. 16, No. 3 (1974).

Cambridgeshire in the 1920s and '30s, has been realised in practice by the establishment of twenty-two such colleges in Leicestershire. The school operates, therefore, as part of an institution having much wider and more various functions than is usual; these extend and enrich those of the school as a neighbourhood school and are in line with developments in other parts of the country where the community function has been built into the comprehensive idea as a natural, cohesive development. The building was designed to include facilities for youth and adult community activities on a single site; but there were other considerations affecting the final design of the building which originated in the experience of comprehensive education.

Instead of the usual rows of box-like classrooms, Leicestershire had already begun to erect secondary school buildings on an open-plan basis, allowing for team (or co-operative) teaching and individual and group activities of various sizes as well as class or larger groupings. This concept was based on the resources approach to learning, which represented a shift from class teaching as the normal mode to individual and group work and what is sometimes called the discovery approach to learning (involving independent learning) – an approach which, at the time Countesthorpe was being planned, was under intensive investigation by the Nuffield Resources for Learning team (of which Tim McMullen, Michael Armstrong and John D'Arcy, the first deputy head, who all took up appointments at Countesthorpe, were members). The then director of education for Leicestershire, Stewart Mason, together with his team, set out to design a building which would both facilitate the 'resources' approach, and also, by means of the circular shape chosen, facilitate interdisciplinary work through the positioning of related disciplines (or activities) such as, for instance, science, technology and design. Separate classrooms were, of course, provided – areas where groups of roughly that size could be located for specific activities; but the main impression on entering Countesthorpe is of the larger teaching areas designed to allow flexible forms of grouping.* (See Figure 1).

Such was the nature of the building erected. It was not, incidentally, unique in Leicestershire. Bosworth College at Desford, Wreake Valley, the Oadby Beauchamp School, were all planned as community colleges and based on new principles of this kind, principles which had emerged from the experience of teaching and learning in comprehensive schools. But Countesthorpe represented the culmination of advanced educational thinking at the stage it was designed. It must also be remembered that the College was planned as an upper school – one taking students from 14 upwards. It embodied, therefore, Stewart Mason's concept of a more

* For a discussion of the principles underlying the new school buildings in Leicestershire see Stewart C. Mason (ed.), *In our Experience* (Longman, 1970), especially pp. 1–29.

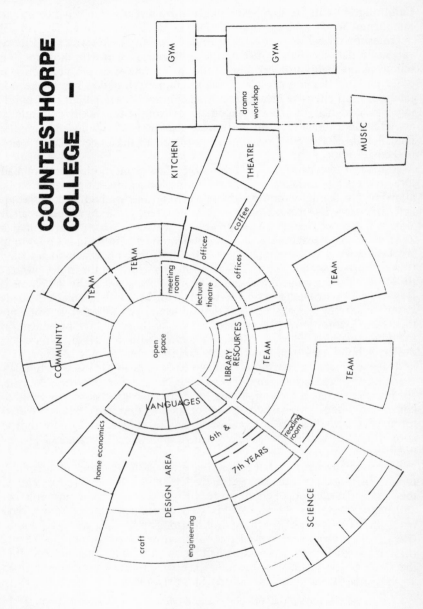

FIGURE 1

mature and so responsible community than would be possible if the age-range 11–18 had to be covered.

The third new development, again arising from the traditions and experiences of comprehensive schools and taking these farther, concerns the form of government or 'constitution' of the school. It had early been realised that, in the large 11–18 (all-through) comprehensive schools, the traditional roles of head and assistant staff were no longer appropriate. Inevitably there had to be devolution of powers – normally from the head to heads of departments on the academic side, and to heads of houses (or 'year-groups') to care for the pastoral responsibilities that were seen to be essential from the start of the movement to comprehensive education. Various forms of more or less democratic (or, more usually, oligarchic) structures developed in comprehensive schools throughout the country in the late fifties and sixties, often involving full staff meetings, departmental meetings, year or house staff meetings, with usually two committees at the top – of heads of departments and heads of houses – who worked directly with the head teacher. All this was clearly a function of the move to comprehensive education – the means by which these schools attempted to involve the full power and energies of the staff in the day-to-day management and long-term planning of the complex variety of activities in a comprehensive school.

It was this tradition that was taken one stage farther at Countesthorpe by the decision of the first principal, Tim McMullen (previously head of the very successful Thomas Bennett Comprehensive School at Crawley) that the school was to be run by the staff as a whole, through discussion and joint decisions arrived at by consensus. The head would participate in the discussions, but would carry out decisions so reached. In other words the head or principal would act, as it were, as chief executive, deliberately subordinating himself to the staff as a whole as regards decision-making.

This step, which, it can be argued, was a logical development from earlier experience, was seen as a means of ensuring that each and every member of the school's staff could feel a genuine, and equal, responsibility for running the school, so that participation and involvement could be maximised. It was originally planned that students would also participate in the process, and, as the older age-groups have built up in the school, they have done so extremely effectively. And this leads on to another very important aspect of the College's work.

This concerns teacher–student relationships generally, and arises from the adoption of the resources approach to learning and its concomitant, the concept of autonomy as an aim of education – the promotion of individual responsibility for learning and for behaviour. This approach also derives from modern educational thinking and experience, both in primary and secondary – perhaps especially comprehensive – schools. In this context the traditional schoolmaster's sanctions relating to punishments (and rewards) as the means of control were not acceptable; through their own experience the students must assimilate norms of behaviour. The school was conceived as a joint enterprise between staff and students as a whole; a new style (or form) of teacher–student relationships was regarded as central to the new conception of learning and development.

Innovations so far-reaching (although in each case the product of the developing tradition and experience of comprehensive schools) could hardly have been brought about simultaneously in an existing school with already established norms of behaviour, of organisation and practice. But in this case here was a new school, with new, specially designed buildings. Staff could be recruited voluntarily, from those ready and willing to accept the new approaches and prepared to participate actively in their realisation. From the start the staff appointed took over their responsibilities, established the staff council (or moot), made their original plans and, in September 1970, the whole enterprise got under way.

It is not my purpose, in this brief introduction, to detail the history of the College during its first five years of existence, nor to go in any detail into the content of activities. All this is effectively covered in the body of this book. I should like, here, only to discuss some of the aspects of the College's activities which seem of particular significance at this stage in the transition to comprehensive education.

First, there can be no doubt whatever that teacher participation in the running of the school has resulted in a strikingly high level of involvement by the great bulk of the staff. In some cases this has meant total involvement – a constant ongoing discussion of new approaches and of the optimal organisational forms felt necessary to realise the school's objectives. Since every member of the staff, including young probationary teachers, is fully involved in these discussions, this has meant that alongside the actual process of teaching and learning which goes on daily in the College, there goes on analysis and interpretation involving educational issues of first importance, the constant objective being to relate the theoretical discussion, which itself arises from practice, back to the practice of structuring learning. Such discussion on the part of the staff was at its maximum at the start of the school, when procedures were being established, and certainly took a great deal of the staff's energies. But what has been impressive to observe during this period is precisely the high commitment of staff to the work of the College. I doubt whether it could be paralleled elsewhere. One main advantage of this, of course, is that staff as a whole arrive at a consensus as to objectives and procedures. The result is that the ethos of the school, which is extremely difficult to define, but of which any visitor is immediately aware, is the resultant of a unified approach.

The second point, which strikes anyone entering the school, is the emphasis on developing new forms of teacher–pupil relations. If learning is seen, to a considerable extent, as a function of teacher–student relations, these must be of such a character as to encourage the sense of responsibility and autonomy of the student – his growing ability to take control of his own learning. Teacher–student relations at Countesthorpe are characterised by a sense of respect, by warmth (hence the use of christian names), and by a recognition that the process of learning involves a transaction between teacher and learner in which, in certain circumstances, the roles may be reversed – an aspect that is acutely developed in Michael Armstrong's article. The close relations between teachers and students at Countesthorpe has, in my opinion, been one of the main factors in winning support among parents for what are admittedly somewhat radical innovations.

The third aspect of the school which is of considerable significance is the successful attempt that has been made at Countesthorpe to develop a unified school – that is, a school in which students are not segregated from each other according to some prediction as to their likely future intellectual development. It has been a main principle at Countesthorpe from the start that streaming, setting and other divisive forms of organisation are no longer appropriate to the new methods of promoting learning which have been adopted. The resources approach calls for individual and group work, as indicated above. From the start, therefore, Countesthorpe has sought to find the means by which all pupils, whatever their so-called 'ability', can be educated together.

Here again Countesthorpe is developing – and taking farther – the movement within comprehensive schools as a whole which, over the last two decades, has increasingly sought the means of developing a unified internal structure, specifically by adopting non-streaming (or mixed-ability teaching) in the early years, from 11 to 14. This approach is difficult to achieve for the 14 to 16 age-groups since the present examination system tends to force a divisive form of organisation on comprehensive (and other) schools. The General Certificate of Education was originally designed for the top 20 per cent of pupils in the 'ability' spectrum. The Certificate for Secondary Education was designed later to cater for the next 40 per cent. The remaining 40 per cent of students were regarded as 'school leavers' for whom no examination was appropriate. Thus a tripartite division was built into comprehensive schools as a result of examination policy.

Countesthorpe has been a pioneering school in its successful attempts to overcome this pattern. This has been achieved by moving over to mode 3 CSE examinations (and utilising the new mode 3 GCE examinations) in such a way as to equate the areas of study in both cases. As a result it has been possible to keep students together during the 14–16 period whether they were sitting GCE or CSE (or, indeed, no examinations). The teachers at the College have developed techniques which enable group and individual learning to be promoted in this situation. This form of organisation has the clear advantage that no doors are slammed on individual students but, on the contrary, all are kept open for as long as possible. The result is that no individual student need automatically feel himself rejected. The fact that Countesthorpe had no problems whatever in assimilating the extra year-group when the school-leaving age was raised in 1974, while schools all over the country certainly experienced considerable difficulties, indicates the success of this approach from this standpoint and is, in my view, greatly to the College's credit.

The fourth point to which I wish to draw attention as a significant new development is the move towards the 'team' approach to teaching, particularly in the fourth and fifth years (14–16). This approach is described in detail in 'Schools Within Schools', and in Dave Claiden's article. Its essence lies in the division of each year-group into two sub-groups each of about 120 students, the central core of whose education is in the hands of a team of six teachers, covering various subject areas. These teachers are responsible for both the academic and the pastoral side of the work. The system has, therefore, led to the fusion of these two aspects of the teacher's responsibilities in a comprehensive school, aspects which until now have been kept separate. The large comprehensive school has many advantages, and much attention has been given to the best forms of pastoral care within such schools by means of the house or the year-group system. Nevertheless, large schools do have their problems, and a good deal of attention is now being given to the advantages of smaller units in education. The Countesthorpe team approach, by which the students follow the basic core of their education with the team of six teachers, combining this with options done outside the team areas, is a means of developing what is sometimes called a 'school within a school', that is, a smaller unit within the school as a whole to which both staff and students can feel a genuine sense of belonging. It is, perhaps, early days to evaluate this experiment, but it seems to give stability to both the students and the staff, and certainly provides one means by which large schools might be broken down to smaller but still organic units within the school. This approach is now being tried out in other schools, both in Leicestershire and elsewhere – indeed, there is a general movement in this direction. This also is something which has been pioneered at Countesthorpe.

The fifth aspect has already been referred to: that is, the development of the resources approach to learning, and the consequent stress on individual and group work. The objective here is the promotion of independent learning and Countesthorpe is now a centre for developmental activities relating to this approach under the aegis, particularly, of Eric Green, head of the science department. This has meant the consistent development of new techniques of promoting learning, in particular the use of work cards, or assignments, and of other methods of arousing the motivation of students and their ability for independent work. This matter is dealt with in a number of the articles in this book, particularly in Jeff Shapland's paper 'Individualised Learning in Science'.

There are, no doubt, many other aspects of Countesthorpe which might be referred to, and those singled out for comment here might be regarded as arbitrarily chosen. Nevertheless enough has been said to indicate the extent of the new approaches embodied at the College, and the seriousness with which the whole enterprise is being undertaken. As I indicated earlier, one of the most impressive things about the College is the way in which the staff have carried out their work relatively undisturbed by what can only be described as an unscrupulous campaign against the College by the local press and in other ways. It is not surprising that innovations of this character should give rise to conflicts. One particular difficulty that the College experienced was the resignation of the first principal due to ill health after five terms. When appointed as the second principal, John Watts had a difficult row to hoe. However, this he has done triumphantly, so that today one can say without doubt that the College has won the massive support of the parents – an outcome partly due to the nature of student–teacher relations, and more recently to overcoming the natural anxieties of parents concerning examinations and their children's future careers. Examination results in the last two years, covering O level GCE and CSE Grade I passes per head, are now clearly above the national average, while many leavers have now passed into universities, polytechnics, colleges of education, into other forms of further education and into local employment. Of course mistakes have been made at various times, but with the support of the local authority, the early difficulties have now been overcome, and the College, having weathered the storm, is still pursuing its original objectives as an integral part of the local community. Any other outcome would have meant a serious defeat for education.

As suggested at the start of this introduction, Countesthorpe is a unique school. Because it was a new school, it was able to put into practice, and take farther, a number of new trends or traditions in education emerging from within the general movement to comprehensive education – to fuse and crystallise these within a new structure. Such a step is really only possible where a school, embodying new objectives, is designed and then supported by its local authority, so that appropriate staff can be appointed from the start. It would not be possible to introduce innovations on so wide a scale throughout the school system in this way. But, I would contend, the school is of value as a prototype of the school of the future. Embodying, as it does, a variety of contemporary trends in educational thinking and practice, it provides a means by which these can be tested out in practice. This, surely, is to render an important service to education.

What effect has the setting up of Countesthorpe had on the rest of the school system – in particular on the new developing system of comprehensive schools? This, of course, is impossible to gauge with any accuracy, and in any case it is still too early to attempt an assessment. Nevertheless is there as an example, visited by many teachers from this country and abroad, as well as by administrators, students and others. Already teachers from Countesthorpe have been appointed as heads (2), deputy heads (3) and to other senior positions in other schools; several have moved to lectureships in colleges of education or universities, one as a local authority adviser.

It is in this intangible way that the influence of Countesthorpe will make itself felt throughout the school system. I think it could be argued that, just as Thomas Arnold's Rugby provided the model for the expanded system of 'public' schools in the mid to late nineteenth century, so Countesthorpe may provide the model for the new type of maintained school arising a century later – that is, the comprehensive secondary school developed to meet the needs of the great majority of the children of this country. Countesthorpe embodies a cohesive approach to education. Its form of organisation, content and methods of teaching and learning and general ethos, are all organically related and form a unity. The principal and staff of the College would be the last, as I knew well, to present themselves as a model for other institutions. In any case, involved as they are in the continuing search for the most appropriate forms and procedures, they would repudiate any suggestion of finality. But there is no question, in my mind, as to the significance of the school's establishment for the future education in this country.

This book, contributed to by staff, students, parents and others concerned in various ways, effectively sets out the grounds for this judgement, and should make the College's experience much more widely available than hitherto.

It was not until October 1973 that Countesthorpe was able to operate with its intended age-range 14–18. Until then it had had to incorporate 600 children aged 11 to 13. When the buildings of the Leysland School were available, this element moved over to them with their own headmaster. At this point the upper school was given a full inspection by the Department of Education and Science. In the normal way, the school presented written statements of aims and practice in each area of work. What may be interesting about the following opening statement is not only its content but its mode of drafting. Although a first draft was made by the principal, it was discussed in moot, amended, and finally agreed as a document to which all the staff subscribed. Though details of record need updating, it stands unaltered as a declaration and may be worth relating to the statement made nearly two years later, on p. 156.

2

General Statement of Position
Endorsed by the Moot, October 1973

Countesthorpe College opened in 1970 with a stated intention by its staff and principal to serve the identifiable needs of its students for the present and future. This did not imply a rejection of the past so much as a resolve to question any established practice for its validity in these terms instead of continuing it automatically. It was recognised that if teachers failed to ask such questions, the young were already doing so.

Because of this increased questioning on the part of the young, it is felt that the key to successful learning, under any heading, is going to be found in the student's own motivation. This motivation might be internal, arising from the desire to achieve understanding and to produce successful outcomes of work, or it might be external, arising from the desire to pass examinations, to progress towards a satisfactory job, to please family, teachers or friends. In either case, learning is recognised as an outcome of relationships that will increase such motivation, and the basis of this is in the recognition of the teacher as an accessible, trusted adult.

With this eye to present and future needs, any approach to learning must take into account such factors as the explosive growth in the sum total of human knowledge and the increasing mobility of people in their work, dwelling-place and general human contact. A static body of common knowledge forms only a very limited part of necessary information, and children now acquire a high proportion of this from such sources as television and travel. The school curriculum is consequently less concerned than formerly with how teachers impart knowledge than with how learners obtain it, select from it and use it. We have seen the teacher in the role, therefore, more as organiser of situations in which learning may occur, one who poses or identifies problems that students will be motivated to solve, one who heightens that motivation and one who imparts the skills for solving these problems.

The knowledge needed by the adolescent student seems above all to include knowledge of the self and of the relationship of self to the environment, socially and physically. The skills of obtaining and employing this knowledge are seen to include logical skills (analysing, generalising, synthesising), communication skills, creative and expressive skills. They relate to the social skills that make it possible to collaborate with others and carry through undertakings to successful conclusions.

It is with these aims in mind, the maximum achievement of each individual's potential and, increasingly as he grows up, each individual's taking the responsibility for that achievement, that Countesthorpe developed its form of architecture, curriculum, personal relationships, style of teaching, organisation for learning and internal government. Above all, it is felt that in a comprehensive school, these aims, to be valid, must apply to *all*. The architecture, with its wheel of interrelated areas for learning, large open areas and group areas of varying size, can be best understood from the plan and through the feet.

The student selects from the possible combinations of the curriculum with the guidance of staff in such a way that an individual's timetable may be unique. The teachers will have in mind a concept of the balanced curriculum and a practical application of it to the individual student's capacity and interest, but they will relate this to the student's expressed interests, so that the agreed programme will be the result of a negotiation (hence the need for access to teachers and full opportunity for developing the skills of negotiation). How this has led to our system of teaming in the upper school is outlined in another section. Certainly, the need for all students to find access to teachers and to know them as trusted adults has led to a loosening of the formalities that often form a barrier between student and teacher. We have abandoned the staff-room as a separate social area. Staff have a number of small rooms for some privacy in preparation and storage, but the general social area, used by day and evening, allows for a high degree of contact between staff and students.

The general aims and the architecture lead to a style of learning that is centred on work based upon problems, posed by teachers and often by the students themselves, and carried out by the students individually or in small groups. There are times when larger groups form, for presentations or instruction, but the small group is the basic unit for study. The study may be expressive, creative, or it may need to draw on the resources made available by the staff. These resources, including library books, and other papers, audio-visual equipment, materials prepared and printed by staff, and of course the staff themselves, are made available in ways described in more detail elsewhere.

Our system of internal government, in which every member of staff and the student body has a part that can be taken, derives from the system of learning. The more a student takes responsibility for studying, the more a student will need a voice in determining the conditions of study: the more teachers are expected to co-ordinate their implementation of curriculum, the more they will need to determine the organisation of the available resources and distribution of responsibilities.

The external provision for our College is made by the Leicestershire County Council. It determines our comprehensive nature, our establishment as a community college, the catchment area and age of entry, it allocates the finances on which we run, and maintains the building and site. Our main intermediary in seeing that these provisions are carried out is the governing body. Its membership includes representatives of the community council, and staff have two representatives who attend meetings. (From February 1975 two teachers, elected by staff, have full voting membership of the governing body.) With the local education authority it appoints the college principal who is held responsible for the curriculum and conduct of the College. The moot and the community council formulate the College's policy. The principal, as well as playing a full part in policy-making through the moot, the committees and the community council, acts with his deputies as chief executive. In the light of existing LEA practice the moot recognises the special responsibilities of the principal representing the College to the outside world, in particular the governors, the LEA and the local community. The moot is open to all staff, students in so far as they wish to attend, and parents when they are able. The community council is a body representing each class or group of users within the adult and youth provision of the College. The moot meets about once a month and the community council about once a term.

The moot forms sub-committees, standing or *ad hoc*, to deal with specific business. The principal standing committee meets once a week to consider points at issue, to advise the executive, set up its own working parties and to determine when a matter affecting basic policy requires a moot to be called. The principal and deputies attend all meetings to give and take advice. The day-to-day business of the school is undertaken as appropriate by the principal, deputies, the administrator, the staff as tutors, year-teachers and heads of departments.

At this point in time it is possible to say that this system, though still developing, has stabilised. This stability is felt to be crucial to the student's capacity to learn. It has come about with a growing awareness on the part of students that their teachers carry authority in their function as teachers without appearing to be authoritarians. This implies that the teacher will need to lay down certain prerequisites for learning even though he is open to negotiation over what is to be learnt. It also implies that certain constraints expected by the watching public, parents and others, must be respected if the goals of the school are to be achieved. These things we recognise.

The start of public examinations in 1972 has also affected student attitudes towards study. With advantage it has provided additional motivation: but for many it has created a situation where non-examined activities are undervalued and rejected. On the other hand, two years of results at GCE O level and in CSE, respectable if not generally spectacular, have given confidence to students and their parents where any of them had suspected that the more tangible dividends might not be forthcoming. (If not *generally* spectacular, it might nonetheless be worth noting two points. One fifth former found it possible this summer to pass eight subjects at O level at Grade 1. And, for reasons probably to be found in the possibilities for expressive exchange in the school as a whole rather than solely in its English teaching, about half of the total comprehensive intake both years passed GCE O level in English.)

Finally, it should be stated that our development is dynamic, has not reached and is unlikely to reach a static, perfected arrangement, for one main reason: the initiative for change may come freely from any source rather than solely from the top. There is good evidence to show that the more hierarchic an organisation is, the more resistant it is to change. Our system facilitates the expression of anyone's inventiveness, staff or student. This does not mean that we plunge headlong from one random innovation to another. Far from it. Proposals need to be carefully presented, will then be critically examined in working parties, experience will inform the judgements passed, modifications almost invariably are made and consensus needs to be reached before implementation. This has the advantage of enabling everyone to feel that they really can affect the working of the College and of committing them consequently to the policy and practices adopted as a result of the process.

There is, however, another side-effect of this system that merits observation, though it is probably not a disadvantage in the long run. It is that we appear, even at times to ourselves, to be a disputatious lot. We readily air our disagreements and criticise each other's views, expecting and taking for granted the high degree of mutual tolerance this requires. Because we also take for granted now a high level of agreement on overall aims, we may sometimes fall prey ourselves to the passing belief that we are racked with schisms. This is not really so. It is another outcome of our openness that our differences are laid bare, because we believe that only in this way will attitudes and practices be modified so as to bring us to a consensus.

Currently we are looking closely at the relative functions of the teacher within the team and the specialist working in a subject department. We are looking again at our policy on examination entry. We now have enough experience under our belt to explore the relative merits of resource material and teacher–student discussion of whether the two-year examination run, 14–16, is the fairest for our students and whether for many a three-year run would not be better. We are uncertain still as to the best way, in sheer mechanics, to organise a timetable so as to facilitate multiple choice for the maximum number of students. We frequently reconsider (who doesn't?) the ways of improving communications, internal and external.

But only a superficial hearing of these debated issues could suggest polarisation among staff, even on an isolated issue, let alone over their sum total. What we can lay claim to, with some pride, is an open dialogue on the real concerns, a confirmed belief that only out of such continuous dialogue will the acceptable way forward continue to be found, and that the context for the dialogue is a strong body of shared commitment. This commitment can be summed up by stating that we regard all our students of equal value but each one as having unique needs and capabilities; that we attempt to cater for this uniqueness so as to do justice to each student in terms both of personal, social development and of qualification for employment and continuous education; that as an essential part of the process, we should guide all our students towards the goal of accepting responsibility for their own actions, to achieve moral autonomy. A centrally held belief can be the least often stated because it seems obvious to its holders: these declarations may be worth making as a statement of what binds us together at Countesthorpe.

3

Countesthorpe College — the First Five Years

VIRGINIA MAKINS

VIRGINIA MAKINS, as deputy editor of The Times Educational Supplement, *has followed and reported on Countesthorpe since before the time when it opened. She has visited the College regularly and also consulted parents, members of the governors, education officers elected members of the Leicestershire County Council. In May 1975 the* TES *published two articles which followed a series of longer visits earlier in the year. In them Virginia Makins surveyed the five years' experience in the fullest form published at that time.*

The PTA committee immediately requested and financed the reproduction and distribution of the articles to all parents, both its own members and, with the support of local head teachers and their staffs, all parents in the contributory schools.

The articles are reproduced from The Times Educational Supplement *by permission.*

THE STORY OF COUNTESTHORPE

'We have a chance to rethink the total process of learning within a school, subject only to the demands made by outside institutions – i.e. universities and parents – and the personal and material resources available to us. This does not mean that everything we do will be different from what has been done before, but it should mean that we do not automatically repeat an established practice without considering why.'

Tim McMullen, 1969

When Countesthorpe opened five years ago this autumn, there was nothing modest or tacit about its aims. Tim McMullen, the first 'warden', hand-picked a staff for innovation. The building had been designed to the specification of one of the most adventurous education authorities in the business, with large open-plan carpeted spaces and a centrepiece sculpture by Phillip King. Radical intentions were widely broadcast – by the *TES* among others – and the school, from the start, inspired a good deal of national and international interest.

However much other schools, which believe they have been working along the same lines but more quietly, may deplore the fact, many people will judge a whole set of trends in secondary education – towards a freer curriculum, wider participation in the running of schools, the abandonment of old rituals and the move to new styles of teacher–pupil relations – by the successes or failures of Countesthorpe. And since the school has been unable to take all the thousands of teachers who have wanted to visit it (and many of its hostile critics have never asked to visit it) it is important, at this stage, to take a close look at what has been achieved.

These two articles attempt to give a brief outline of what has happened at Countesthorpe, both internally and in terms of public reaction, to describe how the school is working now that, as most parents and pupils will tell you, it has 'settled down', and to indicate some of the large questions the whole story raises about the curriculum and organisation of secondary schools, the possibilities and desirability of change, the professional freedom of teachers, the control of schools and the problems of parental choice and influence.

The school was planned as an upper school for 1,440 14 to 18-year-olds, and a community college. In terms of curriculum, the first plans were *avant garde* but by no means unique – integrated social studies, arts linked with crafts, English with drama and music, and so on. Every student was to follow a core curriculum, there would be lots of options and an increasing amount of 'independent time' as students got older. Streaming was out, resource-based individualised learning was the thing, and there was considerable determination to give equal attention and resources to every child, and not to allow those taking GCE to have more than their fair share.

The organisation was fairly conventional for a large comprehensive, with faculty heads to look after the academic side, year heads to handle the pastoral side, and tutor groups. What was unusual was the determination of all staff to remove all points of staff–student friction that had nothing to do with learning and teaching. There was a pretence of a non-compulsory uniform, thanks to parental pressure, but few students or parents paid attention. Students were to be allowed into the staff-room at any time, and there were no separate staff lavatories. Almost everyone easily moved to christian-name terms.

Where Countesthorpe moved far beyond what other schools were doing was in decision-making. All decisions were to be made by the 'moot' of teachers, non-teaching staff, and eventually such parents and older students as wanted to attend. Appointments, allocation of resources and salary points were all awarded by committees appointed by the moot, and the head was bound by their decisions. Quite soon, it became clear that moots were too unwieldy for everyday decisions, so the staff divided into four rotating standing committees to run the school. But any decision could be challenged, and a moot called.

The most unconventional aspect of the school worked the best. The moots laid themselves open to much mockery, there was endless circular talk – but the talk often led to clear decisions, and more or less everyone felt involved in them. There was a milestone when several parents came to a crucial moot on smoking policy and agreed to allow smoking, but to corral it in a small section of a coffee bar for staff and students.

A good deal of in-service education in school management went on when it came to allocating resources. This took a good deal of time at first, but decisions were ultimately based on exhausted consensus, and welded the staff together behind the purposes of the school. So the early rhetoric began to be worked out in practice.

But in the second year, moots became increasingly concerned with failures on the academic and pastoral side. The core curriculum/option system simply did not work – at least not for the 14-year-olds who only had a couple of terms of their school life to run. Children wandered around the school, no one knew where they belonged or where to send them, teachers were too wary of resorting to old authoritarian methods. Gradually, damage and graffiti increased until the look of the school seemed to justify the most hostile headlines in the *Leicester Mercury*.

Part of the trouble was undoubtedly that the teachers had been over-ambitious and over-optimistic about how much they could lay on in terms of fairly individualised curriculum options, in a brand new school which was innovating on all fronts. The school's modern reprographic machinery purred away, producing endless worksheets – but their quality was variable, and even when they were good, it rapidly became clear that a worksheet-based curriculum was a pretty dreary affair. There was no time for proper planning of courses, the resources were poorly co-ordinated, and one suspects for the non-exam students the menu ended up like a poor Chinese restaurant – apparent variety, but everything tasting the same.

To some extent this was offset by the excellent and developing teacher–pupil relationships. Against mounting public pressure, the staff's nerve held when it came to avoiding arbitrary rules and sanctions. Some would say that they carried it to extremes – the example always given is that children are allowed to play transistors in school. But the staff stuck to their guns : 14-year-olds who had already rejected school, they maintained, would only start learning by their own choice, because they liked the place and had formed a positive and trusting relationship with a teacher. The kinds of sanctions most schools apply could only prevent this from happening.

It is important to emphasise that, throughout this time, the traditional academic business of a school was developing in terms of GCE and CSE courses, and that the option scheme provided reasonable protection for children who wanted to study. The remedial scheme was devoted and excellent, with a team moving out of their base to help children with difficulties to get through a normal curriculum.

And there were plenty of children with difficulties. In the beginning McMullen had somewhat recklessly gone out of his way to announce that Countesthorpe was to be really comprehensive, and to attract children whom other schools might have suggested needed special schooling. Its normal intake consists of a fully comprehensive group from the county, and a group from a Leicester housing estate which has been creamed by city grammar schools, and contains its share of pretty difficult city children who, by 14, have been convinced that schools have nothing to offer them.

But as the physical appearance of the school deteriorated, parental and political hostility increased, fanned by sensational publicity. The publicity rubbed off on the children, who faced endless arguments at home and outside about the school. When I visited Countesthorpe at the end of the second year I heard two fourth-year boys talking about an incident that day. 'We was walking down the lane at dinner time, and there was a man with a dog, and he says : "That school ought to be set on fire, it's a place for criminals." It's not like that – it's a minority who go round smashing things up, and most people do lessons, and what he said was a load of rubbish – but you don't look for trouble so we didn't say nothing.'

Some of the hostility can be traced to the personality and poor health of Tim McMullen who disliked confrontation and risked appearing tense and arrogant when dealing with opposition. There is no doubt that while he was extremely successful in getting across the aims of the school to the national and international education world, he failed dismally with his local constituency. And the teachers were too busy getting the place running to do the job.

Under increasing illness and strain, McMullen resigned in the fourth term. Many teachers thought it was the end – the authority and governors would never appoint another head who would stick to the democratic organisation of the school. They were wrong : the job went to John Watts, an experienced head, who emphasised at his interview that he stood squarely behind McMullen's conception of the school.

Watt's public personality could hardly be more different from McMullen's – he exudes confidence and reassurance. He announced to the staff that he would get on with improving the school's public relations, while they developed the school. But he made it clear he was not going to pussy-foot about objectives, in the interests of a quiet public life. In an early paper (the history of Countesthorpe is littered with papers, by staff and, more recently, by a few students) he wrote :

'If our objective is to assist the students to take increasing control of their own destinies, to question assumptions, to solve problems by being inventive and trained to envisage speculative alternatives, we are bound to meet conflict within an industrial society that sees schools principally as the sorting house for employment.

Even among those who have looked closely enough to realise that we have not just sold out to students, that they do not do as they please, that a continuous dialogue of guidance exists, there are many who will object because the teachers are failing to dictate the fields of study, failing to instil a sense of respect for the respectable, failing to establish an institution whose form of government implies an unquestioning obedience to authority.'

When Watts joined, the way had already been charted, so far as internal organisation was concerned. From the first year the debate about what to do with 'non-involved' students had become more intense. Some, including Tim McMullen and John D'Arcy, his deputy, had come to think that the way ahead was to keep the basic organisation, but increase and enrich the options for non-academic students. Some specialist teachers had wanted to abandon the idea of a 'core' curriculum altogether.

Others – including Michael Armstrong, whose articulate, creative and intellectual approach to curriculum has been crucial to the development of the school, and Di Griffin (then head of the remedial operation, and soon to be second deputy head), whose practical and experienced determination to have the school work has been an important sheet anchor in the storms – had wanted a total change of organisation. The last group had proposed the idea of breaking the school up into 'minischools', with teams of teachers taking full responsibility for the pastoral and academic care of groups of 120–50 students.

They had argued that if the school was to meet its fundamental principle of developing the autonomy of students in directing their own studies, teachers must know both their subjects and their students well. And teachers needed to be positive, forceful and ambitious in their expectations of students.

'We have neither sufficiently demonstrated to students the strength of our own commitments, values and interests, nor have we shown sufficient regard for theirs', they wrote. The key problem was the separation of pastoral and academic matters – you cannot guide students unless you get to know them really well by teaching them.

'We need to look for ways of placing the pastoral system at the centre of the learning system of the school, without destroying the excitements and opportunities of specialisation.' Teachers would get to know students 'not just as people, but as learners, and not just in one subject, but across the curriculum'.

So the 'team' idea, which is perhaps Countesthorpe's most significant contribution to ideas about secondary organisation and curriculum, evolved. Incoming fourth-year students were divided into the 'teams', manned by teachers mainly from the 'core' disciplines of English, social studies and maths. Those three fields were covered in 'team time', taking up about half the week. Each team teacher had a tutor group, and was 'directly and immediately and continuously responsible' for the social and academic progress of his or her students. In the rest of the time, students would take options that could not be fielded by the teams. But there were no hard and fast timetable distinctions: students negotiated individual timetables, but if they could not be persuaded to sign on for options (or other teachers wanted to get rid of them) the team areas were manned to look after them.

This proposal was not accepted without a fight. It was endlessly discussed in the spring term of the school's second year. Finally, when the advocates of the team had given up hope, Di Griffin went round the staff asking who would like to try teaching in a team that autumn, and put forward to the moot a short specific proposal with names of teachers, including mathematicians, for two fourth-year teams. It was accepted.

So the third year began with a new organisation that was to be crucial and highly successful in 'settling down' the school. By that time a great deal of damage had been done in terms of parent and public confidence. There was genuine and reasonable concern of parents whose children were at the school, or about to go. Many were concerned because, for the first three years, Countesthorpe was taking younger children than the organisation was designed for. The upper school is part of a campus which also includes an 11–14 high school, but the younger children were housed in the upper school while the high school was being built. It was a sensible economic plan; but it compounded the difficulties of starting up a radical school for older secondary students.

The worries eventually found expression in a petition by 411 people – not all of them parents – demanding that their children should be given suitable and efficient education under the 1944 Act. The publicity this received led 920 parents to sign a statement expressing strong support for the staff, and deploring the sensational publicity the school had received since the beginning. But the first petition was welcome fuel for the opponents of the school whose concerns were not just educational, but also tied up with local politics.

Local government reform was imminent. It was clear that education – in particular the reorganisation of Leicester city schools – was to be the big issue that the new Leicester–Leicestershire council would have to tackle. The more sensational publicity could be drummed up about Leicestershire's famous two-tier comprehensive system, the better it suited some people in the city. Countesthorpe, and to a lesser extent another new and progressive upper school, Wreake Valley, became the targets. The publicity deplored by most parents and students continued, and finally led the chairman of the education committee to ask Mrs Thatcher for a full inspection of Countesthorpe. Then, when morale was already low, the school had an accidental disaster – a major fire, which took out the administration and resource areas.

So when Mrs Thatcher gave the go-ahead and the team of HM inspectors arrived in October 1973, the high school had been out of the building for just three weeks, and the upper school was operating partly in temporary buildings. The new academic and pastoral organisation had been operating for one year, and the sixth form was only in its second year. Not surprisingly, the Inspectorate were pretty unhappy about the job.

A heavy veil of secrecy, pinned down by Crown copyright, is drawn over the workings of full inspections, and their results. (The school and the governors asked that the report should be published, but the DES refused.) The staff seem to have found the long discussions with individual subject inspectors extremely helpful and often supportive, but the whole occasion somewhat bizarre. The careful rituals of an inspection, no doubt evolved in the interests of maximum discretion, sat uncomfortably in a school where everything was deliberately made open to staff and students. And specific things, like the timetable analysis the inspectors use, could not be made to fit the very individual timetable.

When the report came out in June 1974, the *Leicester Mercury* leaked some of it, giving a fairly balanced report as far as the facts were concerned under disaster headlines. This led the local authority to hold a press conference which revealed the main findings. The inspectors had found the school was excessively dirty and damaged, but reported that they noticed no incidents of violent behaviour or theft. Attendance 'compared well with many schools'.

Good standards had already been achieved in some subjects, and many others showed promise. They found GCE exam results neither better nor worse than they would have expected at that stage of a new school's development, and were confident that they would improve. CSE results were generally sound and in some cases impressive. They found exceptional warmth and trust between staff and students.

At the press conference, it became clear that specific accusations that had been made about political bias in the teaching, lack of attention to religious education and violent and criminal behaviour by students had in no way been borne out by the inspection. Nor did the inspectors criticise the way the school was organised, with its collective decision-making and radical system for appointing staff. What the report did say was that too many innovations had been carried out at the same time, putting the school in jeopardy.

In calling for and getting a full inspection, the critics of the school had done their worst. The education committee set up a sub-committee to investigate the school further (they are still at work). But the mass meetings of parents to discuss the report overwhelmingly supported the school (the parent–teacher association and the governors had already made loyal and supportive statements, the governors saying that many things criticised by the inspectors had already been put right). Hostility at the parents' meeting was mainly directed at the reporter from the *Mercury*.

Most parents were by now inoculated against sensational publicity about the school. A solid effort had gone into informing them about what was happening, and the visible effort that, from the start, and staff had put into solving the problems of individual children and keeping in touch with their parents was beginning to pay off. One major local worry – that Countesthorpe students would somehow be unfit for employment – vanished as it became clear that all leavers were getting jobs, that good relations with employers were being developed, and that the sixth form were successful in getting higher education places.

And the full inspection report had one positive result – last summer the local authority put in hand repairs and redecoration, many of them needed since the summer of 1972. That simple action had a huge effect on the morale of staff, students and parents. The school looked good for the first time since its first year (it still does).

All through the fourth year, the staff and students felt they were being asked to defend themselves against accusations which, when valid, went back to events in the first two years of the school. They really felt that the school was working better than ever before. One large factor in the early troubles had been that the school population was 11 to 14, with the biggest and most powerful students the disaffected fourth years. It was only when the high school moved out and a sixth form had grown up that the school could really begin to work as it was planned.

A side-effect of all the troubles was that the community side of the school developed somewhat separately from the rest. Good things have happened – there are holiday activities for children, there is a creche for mothers while they use some of the facilities of the school, a community council is well established and there is a wide range of evening activities. Countesthorpe has been remarkably successful in integrating parents in the normal activities of the school, both arts activities and GCE O and A level courses. But the main effort of the school and staff as a whole, as opposed to the special community staff, has been to get the upper school going.

The early history of the school raises some uncomfortable questions. One of the most obvious is about parental choice. Should parents virtually be forced to send children to a school that sets out to be different?

But if the experiment has validity, it is mainly because it has been proved to work for most of a comprehensive intake – there is plenty of evidence that progressive schools suit a self-selected minority. If it is professionally irresponsible for schools and teachers to subject children to change for its own sake, it is equally irresponsible to try to maintain a system that is failing to educate many children, simply because the public distrusts change.

If – as will clearly be the case in the foreseeable future – most parents have very little choice between secondary schools, how much attention schools should pay to specific wishes of parents is an important question. There are obvious criteria that must be met, particularly in terms of exam results, which determine the life chances of students. But provided social behaviour and academic results are at least average, how far should teachers, as professionals, be able to experiment in order to try to improve the education of all children, both academic and non-academic – and, indeed, to try to break down that rigid and destructive distinction?

There is no doubt that Countesthorpe, in the first couple of years, asked parents to take too much on trust: it needed a long process of discussion to make it clear what it was trying to do. But how far it could have succeeded in persuading parents that its ideas might work, before trying to put them into practice, is another matter.

In an important sense, for parents and children, the proof of the pudding has been in the eating. Students frequently say to you: 'My mum and dad still don't like it much, but as long as I'm happy, and doing all right they put up with it.' And many parents who signed the original petition are now reconciled to the school: they say their demands have largely been met.

Calls for 'accountability' – and there have been plenty in Leicester during the Countesthorpe saga – are fine if they mean long-term accountability in terms of schools producing results that are acceptable to the public, whether parents, employers or universities. But too much attention to parents' wishes – in matters ranging from uniforms and rules and corporal punishment to teaching methods and homework – may well, in fact, prevent teachers doing the best possible job of educating the greatest possible number of children.

One irony of the story is that the only traditional element left in the management of the school – the governing body – in fact saved the original conception from defeat. Countesthorpe was lucky: its governors, and in particular the chairman, Dr Geoffrey Taylor, have been exceptionally resolute through the troubles. They had an early chance to compromise when McMullen resigned, and refused, appointing a successor determined to see through his policy, and standing behind him during all the troubles.

Some original members of staff blame the initial blast of publicity for some of their troubles; in particular, they say it set others in the Leicestershire school system against the school. John Watts maintains that it would have been very difficult to carry on in the teeth of all the local opposition had there not been a constant and mainly admiring flow of visitors to the school from the rest of Britain and from abroad.

The most important question is the one raised by the HMI's report – did Countesthorpe try to do too much too quickly and, by innovating on all fronts, jeopardise the success of the experiment? There is a tendency among fairly friendly people in the Leicestershire authority, and among parents who have become reconciled to the school, to make Tim McMullen the scapegoat for early difficulties. But the most interesting thing about the Countesthorpe story is that there has been no compromise whatever on McMullen's original plans for a school run on the basis of participatory democracy. Where there have been changes, they have been to make the school more radical, and it has been those changes which have helped the school to 'settle down'.

John Watts and the staff firmly believe that if the school had not tried to do everything at once, it would have been prevented from doing much. Certainly 'progressive' schools that have taken things more slowly at the start have aroused as much distrust among parents as Countesthorpe. And the violence of the local political reaction was as much to do with the politics of local government reorganisation as with the degree of radicalism of the school.

The Countesthorpe story has plenty of lessons for schools and authorities who might want to move in the same direction. But the experiment cannot be judged on the painful teething troubles of the school (especially since the most hostile opponents have not been able to use the leaked HMIS' report to prove that the first pupils suffered in educational terms). What matters is where it has got to, now that the school is fairly settled and established.

DIVIDENDS OF CHANGE

It would be absurd to pretend that Countesthorpe is working under typical conditions. The staff were chosen at the beginning to work in new ways and were committed to the ideas behind the school. The population in the catchment area has declined dramatically, and a school that was planned for 1,440 students will, next year, be used by 980 (780 upper school students and the equivalent of 200 full places taken up by high school students using specialist facilities). The buildings were especially designed for flexibility, so it has been fairly easy to rearrange the organisation of the school and introduce an advanced form of team teaching.

But that is not to say that Countesthorpe is irrelevant to ordinary secondary schools. It is easy to forget that the things Countesthorpe is best known for – the democratic system of management and informal staff–student relations, based on avoidance of authoritarian sanctions – were not designed as ends in themselves, but as means to a system where children learnt more and became more autonomous.

After five years they have succeeded in establishing the means. Open and democratic management works, without taking up too much time and energy. Staff–student relations (and, just as important, staff–staff relations) are as good as could be hoped for, and both staff and students seem convinced that the place is working along the right lines. They have invented a framework for curriculum which may still need a lot of development, but which makes it possible to explore fundamental questions about how older teenagers learn and how the traditional subject disciplines that teachers were brought up in can be fitted to different styles of learning.

It still remains an open question whether Countesthorpe will go much farther in working out those large questions. Now the school is working calmly and comfortably, it would be easy to relax, and concentrate on improving the system in terms of conventional measures – exam standards, the variety of options on offer – rather than in terms of the fundamental issues that have always been a part of the debates that have raged at Countesthorpe: how do you assess standards of learning, do the options on offer really come from the needs of the pupils? Michael Armstrong once wrote: 'We half suspect that we are being urged (not consciously) to pay more attention to the appearance of learning and less to the reality.' It is still possible that they will end up doing just that. But the debate, if no longer raging, is still very much there.

The thing that has got the school working calmly is the team system. Countesthorpe takes 14-year-olds from two high schools, one on the same campus which began its life in the same buildings and with the same attitudes, and one more traditional, feeding in children from a city estate in Leicester who have failed the 11-plus. When they arrive they go into teams which stay together through the fourth and fifth years (the sixth form have their own area and tutors). Last year the teams were very small, with four or five teachers and some 120 students; the year before they had seven or eight teachers and some 170 students. It is a way of breaking down a school that, many would argue, was too big in the first place.

The teams are further divided into tutor groups. Tutors organise the core curriculum of their group – English, maths and social studies – within the team, and 'team time' takes up half the timetable. There are a variety of options, covering all other curriculum areas, including PE and outdoor activities, for the rest of the time. Students arrange individual timetables with the guidance of their tutors; if they cannot be persuaded to sign on for many options they stay in the team area and the team tutors do their best to find some work that will interest them.

The result is that the team teachers get to know their students very well, both as people and as learners, in a way that a system of specialist teachers backed by pastoral staff makes almost impossible. Students are given a stable and encouraging base, and almost all of them respond. 'Our students are all very amiable now, and some weren't in the least amiable when they came', said a tutor in a fifth-year team.

Amiability is an important quality, and it may be one of the things that has saved Countesthorpe from the sort of ROSLA trouble some other schools have faced. But the final test of the system is the work. So far as the core subjects go, English and social studies are generally agreed to be going fairly well and maths not well enough. In theory, and sometimes in practice, the mathematicians in the team know the students well enough to gear the content to suit them – long division for those who like it and feel that is what they need, matrices for others. But it isn't easy teaching mixed-ability groups and trying to get some students through an SMP O level.

Some sixth formers I talked to, now working to upgrade their maths because they wanted to go into retailing or accountancy, reckoned the trouble is that for maths you need 'small groups and blackboard-style teaching'. One team is now planning to run maths in much smaller groups, giving students less time but more attention and getting non-mathematician teachers to back up by doing maths with their tutor groups.

It is in English and social studies, and the indistinct boundaries between these subjects and some options, that the system comes to life. But before describing the work it is worth getting the examination record straight. Countesthorpe started with the determination to give students the examinations at 16-plus they needed – but no more. They did not want to divert resources to a multiplication of O level options. (CSEs, particularly mode 3, were easier to accommodate.) So they offered sciences, languages and mathematics, but cut down to English language and one social studies O level. English literature, history, geography and religious education were, as separate examination subjects, to be left to the sixth form.

Since then, after much shopping around examination boards to find O level syllabuses to fit their teaching – usually ones demanding minimum rote learning, a substantial project component and a reasonable element of continuous assessment – they have introduced an AEB world history O level, a Cambridge Board English literature, religious knowledge and a mode 3 O level with the AEB called community studies, which combines study of child development with practical work with children. The shopping around continues at A level. The language department, for instance, are trying to negotiate a mode 3 French A level. Some teachers feel they are beginning to sell out on their original intention to keep O levels to the acceptable minimum. But sixth formers tell you how free the curriculum feels from examination pressures; they say they can take them in their stride without panic.

Three groups of fifth formers have now taken O levels and it is reasonable to expect standards to go on improving as teachers get more experience with the courses. In 1974, on the local authority's figures, 26.97 per cent of the Countesthorpe intake (four-fifths comprehensive from the county, one-fifth 11-plus failures from the city system) got three or more O levels. The 1974 figure for the fully comprehensive county upper schools was 30·06 per cent. In the city's selective system (which has to deal with the usual urban problems) 25·50 per cent got three or more O levels.

Fifty-five of Countesthorpe's first sixth formers stayed on for two years : they left last summer. Forty-seven of them got up to three A levels and twelve went to university, eight to polytechnics and five to colleges of education. Last year 26 per cent of students stayed on into the sixth form; this year 31 per cent are expected to. The ones who have gone into higher education are satisfied with the school. They say they find it easier than their contemporaries to study on their own, and they feel more broadly educated. 'I seem to know as much sociology as the first year sociologists', one science student told me.

So it would certainly be wrong to say – as Leicester's Professor of Education, G. H. Bantock, did at a recent conference – that Countesthorpe had 'abandoned academic goals'. What it has tried to do, not too unsuccessfully, is to abandon academic paper-chases, and combine academic with other goals. The English and social studies work is a good place to look at results. At this time of year fat folders of work are laid out for external O level and cse examiners. The English folders include work from all kinds of subjects – chemistry, biology, an individual interest like ornithology. A lot of the more conventional English, stories and poems, clearly reflect the first-hand experience students get by doing a lot of work out of school, in hospitals and day nurseries and primary schools as well as on work experience.

The social studies folders cover an enormous range of topics – blood sports, local canal history, blindness, sleep and dreams. They show evidence of first-hand research and original thinking (very original in some cases – one boy writing on blindness blind-folded himself for a whole day at home one weekend to see what it was like). It was clear that students had been led to draw conclusions and defend them. An external examiner commented : 'Very few schools are doing this kind of interdisciplinary social studies with mixed ability groups. When they do, the results are usually excellent, and Countesthorpe is no exception.'

What is exceptional at Countesthorpe is the freedom students have to concentrate on one project, or to take a far greater range of work than a normal timetable would allow. A few bright students are getting through an enormous amount, with the guidance of both their tutors and specialist staff. Some students who could in no conventional terms be called bright are doing impressive work in one field that interests them. (I saw a report by a boy who had spent hours watching a male blackbird and its family. It was part of his cse English folder and compelling reading by any standards.) At the other end of the scale, students who come in at 14 hostile to any idea of school work have been lured back by first being allowed to do very little, then to concentrate on one thing that catches their interest.

All this work is done in a very relaxed atmosphere. The teaching and thinking takes a conversational form. There are a lot of jokes. A few people are doing nothing in particular at any given time (as in offices). People are mostly working at things which interest them. And some students feel life in the team (as opposed to more academic specialist options) is a bit of a skive.

'I was lazy last year', said a sixth former who had been trying to catch up on his maths for a career in retailing. His tutor said he had indeed been lazy, in maths, and no amount of persuasion to work harder had any effect. But he had done a great deal in English. 'There are some students who don't do much because tutors have decided that is that way to handle them at a certain stage, and others who don't do much because the tutors have failed. It is hard for outsiders to tell the difference.'

A surprising result of the team system is that the specialist departments – usually the strongest fiefdoms in secondary schools, controlling most undisputed space, equipment, auxiliaries and firepower in timetable battles – are being driven on to the defensive. In some cases the feeling that the main action is elsewhere is leading them to join teams, at least part-time, next year. This is reinforcing a possibility – still at an embryo stage and presenting large difficulties – that teachers might become more generalist. Already English and social studies teachers in teams are fielding each other's subjects, and both are doing some maths. If scientists, PE or arts staff regularly take part in teams, they could also find themselves branching out of their specialist subjects and helping other teachers get work going in their field.

The school offers a range of specialist options, like many big comprehensives at the 14–18 stage. They are perhaps particularly dedicated to mixed-ability teaching, but all option systems lead to some streaming by self-selection. Most departments offer interesting approaches to curriculum and teaching methods. To take just one example, Eric Green, in physics, has taken individual learning through worksheets just about as far as it can go – much too far in the view of some other teachers, who say it puts off all but the most dedicated physicists.

Relations between teams and specialist departments started off uneasily. Students who had liked languages, science, art and craft or sport at their high schools signed on for the options. But others were reluctant to leave the cosy team areas. It has become clear that the best way to lure them out is for their tutors to go with them – but that isn't easy when the team areas have to be manned at all times and a lot of work in the team happens outside school.

Gradually, partly because teachers in teams feel the need to offer more varied activities to reluctant students, informal two-way traffic is developing between some teams and some departments. One group of very unacademic girls do chemistry (under a 'food science' disguise) with their tutor in the laboratory. The specialists get together the materials and introduce them, but the work is done (with a lot of chatting) with the tutor.

It may be that the Countesthorpe system is a bit too cosy: students like to stay with their friends, and the tutors they know well. But it may also be that in a conventional system, shuttling from teacher to teacher, they would simply turn off.

Other team tutors with musical or artistic or craft inclinations are beginning to go out to specialist areas. They work with groups from the team, leaning on the advice of the specialists but better able to keep their students interested or, if necessary, control them because of their special relationship. When they go regularly, they can take responsibility for supervising the specialist areas while the specialists spend time in the teams.

All these initiatives may fizzle out in the face of practical difficulties, not least that of teachers being in two places at once. But the dividends could be enormous – as the limited experience of some of the teachers in teams already shows.

It seems that when relationships with students get really open, teachers can be forced to rethink their subjects. However sensitively they present the concepts they think important to their subject and relate their teaching to students' individual interests, their pupils may simply reject the concepts. Michael Armstrong gives an example: trying to teach sociological concepts of social class. 'The children just won't accept what sociologists take for granted. They give endless counter examples, and the whole accepted notion of social class explodes. The more you try to defend it, the more difficulty you get into.'

He is finding it more useful to think of education not as an attempt to present disciplines and concepts to students in more or less acceptable ways (as it were, the Bruner approach) but as 'a coming together of teacher, pupil and task in a dynamic relationship through which subject matter is reconstructed for both teacher and pupil in the light of their common or collective experience'. The teacher's knowledge of traditional disciplines is crucial to transforming the child's knowledge gained from his immediate experience. But the child's experience and intuition are just as important to the teacher. (See two articles in *Forum for the Discussion of New Trends in Education* Spring 1975, where Michael Armstrong explains his position and gives a long example based on Countesthorpe students' work in a primary school.)

Another teacher, Lesley King, agrees that the Countesthorpe way of teaching has changed her views: 'Not about trivial things, like pop music, but fundamental things like mental health. One student did a long diary working in a mental hospital. We read things together: my views changed, we seemed to be equals. The endeavour couldn't have happened without either of us.'

Michael Armstrong and Lesley King are the first to admit that such breakthroughs are rare and much of the work done is pretty conventional project stuff. But they are convinced that where the work is (as one teacher puts it) 'dull with overtones of trendiness' the way is not back but on. They want to find out more about why students suddenly get interested and what keeps their interest going. And they want to learn much more about good junior school techniques where teachers stimulate a variety of happenings in a variety of media.

Gradually, some teachers in teams are getting students to use more means of expression – drama and art and craft and photography as well as writing and talk. Next year, when chemists join teams part-time, there will be a chance to explore how much science can happen in the team. There are obvious physical limitations: scientists sometimes need their labs and craft specialists their workshops. But it may be that a lot of the lavishly equipped specialist territory in big secondary schools is not really needed to get students learning. If Countesthorpe goes on moving towards 'minischools' within the school – and more specialists taking part in teams is a step in that direction – that is just one question they can explore.

Another important idea they discussed this year was 'vertical' teams taking students of all ages. It is a logical extension of the system and would solve many problems, not least the psychological difficulty teachers face when, after working for two years with one group and setting up close relationships, they have to start all over again with a new bunch of 14-year-olds.

But after the usual Countesthorpe procedures of discussion papers (a sixth former wanted 'vertical teams for vertical people') and meetings, they decided not to start another structural change at this stage. Several people wanted to concentrate on current problems first – how to get more variety in teams; relationships with specialist departments; maths; how to organise things that need larger groups (ranging from netball to drama and English literature); how to oversee curriculum in a system where heads of department have effectively vanished.

Many visitors comment that this sort of thrashing about is all very well, given a dedicated and very able staff. Certainly the battles of the first two years to start the place up and keep it going were totally exhausting. But now, although the staff work very hard in school and after it, they seem remarkably relaxed.

One reason is that a system designed to develop the autonomy of pupils has had the same effect on teachers. It is important to remember that a lot of teachers who are now operating very effectively in the Countesthorpe system came as probationers. Some of them find they have a real problem about where to go next (a number of teachers have left for promotion; Countesthorpe has already provided two heads and three deputy heads). They are used to working in teams, to being able to try out new teaching ideas without long negotiations about timetables, to take groups of students out of school without fuss, to visit parents when they want to without going through a pastoral hierarchy. They have a hand in the allocation of resources between departments, and in appointments. They are used, when in difficulties, to getting quick and informal help from their colleagues in teams or the remedial staff or the principal and deputies.

John Watts, the principal, has written: 'In any stage of our curriculum development, up to half a dozen young teachers are likely to formulate thought-out schemes each worthy of a single director of curriculum. Then there is argument, and the principal's job is no longer to pour oil on troubled waters but to fish in them.' He offers the school not as a blueprint, but 'an example that alternatives are possible and that students and assistant teachers can themselves generate and maintain change without dependence on initiatives from above and without'.

There is no doubt that this autonomy is one result of the democratic system of management, and that the excellent staff–student relations built from the policy of minimal rules and sanctions make it possible for young staff to get on with developing their teaching.

Like all democratic systems, the one at Countesthorpe needs a good deal of vigilance. Fundamental issues still come up. One, which caused a good deal of anger earlier this year and is still unresolved, is whether trade union members should be able to take unilateral decisions – for instance about whether (as they did) to close the school by going on strike – without going through the democratic procedures of the school.

This crisis briefly unveiled another underlying split between staff, which does not affect the teaching and carries no weight in practical discussions of how the school should run, but which possibly might endanger Countesthorpe's development. The vast majority of teachers see the place as important in educational terms. A very few teachers – perhaps three out of sixty – consider that it can be important only if it is part of political movements: what they call, in capital letters, The Struggle. They consider, rightly, that educational and political questions cannot be entirely divorced – but go on from there to reject much of Countesthorpe's achievement on the grounds that it is not aimed directly at influencing institutions elsewhere, at 'collective liberation', and at getting children involved in changing things other than schools.

But to a visitor, the democracy seems to work amazingly well. If anything, there seems to be too much abstract discussion about whether the school is really democratic, diverting energy from important educational issues. The 'executive' – John Watts and his two deputies – get on with the day-to-day running of the school, co-ordinating, advising and dealing with the outside work. They carry a lot of influence in the weekly committee meetings, but are bound by its decisions. Any student can take part in these meetings, and several do. Anyone can propose a moot for general discussion of an issue at any time.

Allocation of resources, appointments and distribution of salary points now work smoothly. The governors have stopped worrying about the system: where they used to want to keep a detailed check on what was happening, they now leave to the school things that most governors are happy to leave to the head.

If the democracy is a success, the staff–student relations are a triumph. It is impossible to spend five minutes in the school without seeing examples of the 'exceptional warmth and trust' noted by HM inspectors. The belief that, at least for older students in compulsory education, old-style sanctions simply do not work and, if anything, exacerbate difficulties, and the determination to work by persuasion and consent, seem to have been entirely justified in practice.

It has been a wearing process trying, for example, to persuade students to confine transistor radio playing to acceptable times and places, instead of simply banning them. But the result – getting rid of a lot of tensions that have nothing to do with the main business of getting older students learning – gives hope to a number of discouraged secondary teachers who have visited the school.

Things like theft and damage still happen (and are dealt with as quickly and effectively as possible). But the teachers have achieved through personal relationships a great measure of control over some pretty difficult students. Every time I have seen a Countesthorpe teacher telling a student to get down off that window or stop being idiotic with those matches, the student has got down or stopped.

Teachers working in ordinary schools must make up their own minds how far the Countesthorpe experiment applies to them. Working on all fronts at once – management, curriculum, abolishing traditional rituals and sanctions – it has got a long way in five years. It has won the reluctant support of all but a handful of parents and the enthusiastic loyalty of all but a handful of students. It has opened up a lot of questions about how learning is organised in secondary schools, and may get farther in trying to find answers.

So, in many important ways, the experiment has been a great success. It remains to be seen how far it can be disseminated. A lot depends on how far people who control schools will be prepared to back teachers who want to try out some of the ideas developed in Countesthorpe, or to work out their own alternatives to deal with some of the widely acknowledged difficulties and failures of secondary schools that Countesthorpe was designed to overcome.

PART II
CARING AND LEARNING

This book does not attempt a balanced survey of the curriculum. As the account of 'teams' should make clear, the exercise of responsible choice, under the guidance of tutors, results in maximum diversity of programmes for students within the range of what the curriculum offers. The curriculum is the sum total of learning experiences made possible by the College, both within its walls and outside, devised by teacher or student or anybody else called upon to offer a service.

The following articles, with their quotations of students' writings, offer a random viewing of work in progress and our reflections upon it. These particular articles are presented because they are available for reprinting.

4

Schools Within Schools

The Countesthorpe 'team' system

MICHAEL ARMSTRONG and LESLEY KING

MICHAEL ARMSTRONG was appointed head of social studies when Countesthorpe opened. He had previously taught at Wandsworth Boys' Comprehensive School and before Countesthorpe opened he was a team member of the Nuffield Resources for Learning project. He is currently preparing a book for Professor Paul Hirst's series in the Routledge Student Library, in which he considers new models of curriculum and the learning process in popular education.

LESLEY KING was appointed to teach in the social studies department when the school opened in 1970. She became a year-teacher the following year, but has worked full-time as a tutor in the second group of teams since 1973.

The following article was prepared jointly by Lesley and Michael for Forum *in the Spring issue 1976. It charts the development of Countesthorpe's characteristic 'team' system after the experience of the first two years, 1970–2. The article also takes up the theme of Michael Armstrong's earlier article for* Forum, *reprinted in the next section of this book.*

'The process of education, at best, implies a dynamic relationship between teacher, pupil and task out of which knowledge is reconstructed, for both pupil and teacher, in the light of a shared experience.'

In the present article we want to describe the academic and pastoral structure by means of which our school has sought to foster the relationship. The article describes what has from the start been known at Countesthorpe as the 'team' system, although the term has always seemed to us somewhat unsatisfactory. To prevent misunderstanding we would point out in advance that the 'team' system has nothing to do with what is normally known as 'team teaching'. It has different origins and a different purpose, and it is to a description of these that we now turn.

The idea of 'teams' – miniature schools within a school – grew out of a sense of dissatisfaction with the school's original curriculum strategy. That strategy sought to reconcile two apparently conflicting principles.

One was the principle of autonomy – that every student should be responsible for determining the choice and direction of his own course of study with the help and support of his teachers. The task we set ourselves was to create the conditions in which autonomy could thrive. We did not intend meekly to submit to each student's passing whims and fancies, for unless teachers are ready to be positive, forceful and ambitious in their expectations of their students they cannot hope to create the conditions for a thriving autonomy. We did intend, as Stuart Maclure of the *TES* once wrote, to try to 'match the education to the pupil rather than blame the pupil for failing to correspond to the kind of education which is on offer'. The second principle was that of a common curriculum – our commitment to the major disciplines of human thought, the traditional forms of knowledge, mathematics, science, the humanities, the arts. We were convinced at the time, and remain convinced, that every student has the ability to pursue knowledge in all these forms, and that our task was to help each student to do so.

At first we sought to reconcile the two principles by insisting that all students spend equal amounts of time studying each of the major areas of knowledge we identified (two to three seventy-minute lessons each of English, the social studies, maths and science) while insisting at the same time that within each area all teachers encourage each student to pursue knowledge in his own distinctive way.

The strategy failed, not so much because it is in principle impossible to reconcile autonomy with a common curriculum (though it is certainly exceptionally difficult) but rather because the context within which learning and teaching took place frustrated whatever attempts at reconciliation we made. We began to see that the context we needed in order to make a success of student autonomy was one in which teachers and students could take part in a kind of continual conversation with each other – not a dialogue, discussion or argument but something more free-ranging, intimate, expressive and egalitarian, that is to say a conversation. Only through conversation, so we felt, could a teacher learn to identify and value the intellectual demands and interests of his students and a student those of his teacher. Only such a context seemed to offer us a realistic hope of reconciling the student's and the teacher's experience and concern.

Yet the context in which we were working at the time did not encourage conversation to any great extent. How could it, when our curriculum strategy entailed so clear a division between a teacher's academic and pastoral roles, between the teaching group and the tutor group? Our organisation, like that of many other comprehensive schools, kept tutorial guidance and teaching apart as distinct activities with separate structures. Guidance was organised through a pastoral system of year-groups and tutors; teaching through an academic system of subject departments and subject specialists. Some tutors never taught their tutorial group. Those who did, taught them no more than one subject and no more than two or three lessons a week.

We needed a way of bringing the pastoral and the academic systems into one. Most students, if they are successfully to direct their own course of study, need sustained and systematic guidance from teachers who have come to know them well by working with them closely for a long time. The tutorial role should therefore be at the centre of the academic system rather than on the periphery. The tutor's job is to work with his students, not just within the area of his own academic specialism but across the curriculum, teaching whatever he himself is most interested in and involving himself in whatever most absorbs his students. The more he participates in the work of his students across the curriculum, the greater his chances of spotting and turning to advantage opportunities for extending and deepening the range of their intellectual and personal concern. And thereby he helps them to direct their own studies successfully.

We did not want to deny the excitement, or even the necessity, of specialisation in secondary education. We knew and accepted that some of us would always be happiest teaching our own special subject to students who had chosen to study it. But we also knew that many of us had to become more than specialists if we were to achieve the academic goals we set ourselves, let alone the pastoral goals. In theory, perhaps, every teacher needs to be both tutor *and* specialist. In practice some teachers combine the roles more easily than others. In any case the two roles are complementary. The tutor needs the specialist to take over where his own enthusiasm or expertise run out. The specialist needs the tutor to provide the supporting framework that enables a student to make sense of specialisation.

This, then, was the background against which we set about reconstructing our curriculum at the end of our first two years. We now divide each year-group of students into units of 100 to 150 students each. Each unit becomes the direct pastoral and academic responsibility of a group of from five to eight teachers. Students and teachers together make up the 'team'. The group of teachers come from differing specialist backgrounds, usually, but not invariably, English, social studies and mathematics. The common factor is their readiness to assume a new kind of teaching role – new, that is, secondary as opposed to primary schools. Their job is to get to know the students in their team (which is usually divided into tutor groups of some twenty to twenty-five students with one tutor), to work with them over a wide range of activities, and to guide and assist their entire course of study within the College. There is no longer a strictly compulsory core of studies which all students have to follow, but it is one part of the tutor's role to help his students to achieve a balanced curriculum involving all the major disciplines. Tutors spend at least half the week with the students in their teams working in one particular area or set of rooms which becomes the team's base, and is as far as possible exclusive to the teams concerned. Thus teachers and students together make up a kind of minischool within the overall framework of the College, semi-independent, close-knit, distinctive in place and character.

For timetabling purposes the work is organised in two halves of ten periods each. One half – colloquially called 'team time' – is spent by the students in their team area working with their teacher tutors. The other half is devoted to specialist activities under the direction of specialist teachers from outside the team. Any student who has no specialist activity to take part in on one occasion or another during the specialist half of the week can remain in his team area working under the guidance or supervision of one or other of his team teachers. Conversely, there have always been students who have spent one or two lessons of team time engaged on outside specialist activities for which they could not otherwise find room on the timetable.

The difference between 'team time' and 'outside specialist activity' is a difference of emphasis. It would be wrong to think of the latter as the time when students study 'subjects' and the former as the time when they don't. It would also be wrong to imagine a sharp division between 'specialist' and 'generalist' teachers. The difference is rather in the kind of relationship between teacher and student and between both teacher and student together and the activities they engage in, that is to say between them and the curriculum.

Within the team the relationship between teacher and student is intended to be as many-sided as possible. The team's overriding objective is to help its students to make sense of autonomy and to put it to use in the expansion of intellect and personality. The teacher tries to get to know each one of his students as well as he can, both personally and intellectually, not simply for the sake of the pleasure of knowing them but in order to help them to develop their own powers of mind and feeling. This, so we feel, he can only do by talking with students, working alongside them, teaching them and learning from them over as many activities and subject matters as he can cope with. Sometimes he will be teaching his own individual specialism, sometimes following the particular interests and concerns of the student, sometimes teacher and student will be working together on activities neither is necessarily familiar with. The teacher has to be ready with his own ideas and responsive to those of his students, over a very broad area of knowledge. The boundaries between 'academic' and 'pastoral', between different 'subjects' or 'disciplines', between 'work' and 'play', between teacher and taught, become, of necessity, elusive and shifting within the team situation.

By contrast, when students work with specialists outside the team, they go primarily to engage in a particular definable set of activities or to study a particular body of knowledge with the help of an acknowledged expert. In this context teachers and taught will probably concentrate more narrowly on the subject in hand. Within the team, such narrow forms of concentration, desirable and necessary though they certainly are in their place, can never form more than one part of the spectrum of teacher's and student's activity.

For all these reasons, team time is hard to pin down in a precise description. In order to suggest something of its character and content, one of us, Lesley King, has looked back over the work of one of her present fourth-year students during the first six weeks of this autumn term and over the period of pre-term preparation when she was getting ready to receive a new group of students entering the school for the first time. What follows is a brief account of just one teacher's experience of working in a Countesthorpe 'team'.

I first met Phil at his middle school at a time when I was really much more concerned with my present fifth-year group's examination work and future prospects. I was interested in my new group but had no time to give them my attention. I talked to Phil for about fifteen minutes, giving him a booklet of basic information and a bus pass application form. The interview was quite a difficult one. He was obviously nervous. His voice was rather throaty and I found myself talking slightly more softly than usual. I remember that he asked no questions but in answer to my query said that he was looking forward to coming to Countesthorpe. I wasn't convinced and asked him if he minded having a woman for a tutor. Some boys resented being landed with the only woman in the team. He said no. I remember little else about the first meeting. My notes, taken at the time and added to that evening, tell me more. Phil doesn't like maths but likes English very much. He reads adventure stories, thrillers and ghost stories. He wants to give up French but might like to begin learning German. He is also interested in what he has heard of control technology and art. He plays softball, table tennis and volley ball. He has an athletics star award. (He didn't tell me this; he was wearing it.) He plays the piano accordion and would like to do some music.

I met him again shortly afterwards when he and the rest came from the middle school to look round our school. I remember being anxious that they should be impressed by the school. I'm always a bit afraid that fifth-year students will show off in that rough way they sometimes do. Then I'll shout, and so on, and so on. I showed my group round the different teaching areas in the school. Afterwards we went back to the 'pod' – the small separate building that was to be our team area – and I explained about it being 'their' area. Then I left them for a bit as they seemed very tongue-tied, and asked one of my present fifth formers to talk to them. He said afterwards that they asked mainly about sport and music. They looked very small. We went for coffee and of course they hadn't any money. I offered money to lend but they daren't say yes. We were all rather shy. Fifth and sixth years looked at us as if we were from another galaxy. I was glad when the time came to get on the coach again. They waved as they left. I have no special memories of Phil except that he was not at all forthcoming. The notes from his middle school gave the following information – address, birth date, reading age (14½), arithmetical age (11). They also mentioned that he was 'able' but 'underachieving', wanted to be a computer programmer, collected matchboxes and played soccer for the school team. The headmaster did not mention him in particular as outstanding or specially worrying.

I later met his parents at the first parents' evening. This was to show the parents around the school and answer general questions, not specific ones about students. Over coffee his parents said that he was not happy at his middle school but felt that our system would suit him better. I was relieved. Until then I had half thought that Phil was not just shy but hostile, to the school or me or both. It was a good evening altogether. There were one or two arguments but they were productive, no useless chit-chat, no 'do you push them enough?' The school looked impressive. I got quite excited for the first time about the next year, although my mind was still crowded with my present group and their work. I began to think that all the other teachers who felt rather dreary about going back into the fourth year (after spending two years with their previous groups) must be crazy. From this time my mind began to dwell more and more on the new group. I made an elaborate record book for next year – name, address, birth date, previous school/tutor, my own notes, annotated school notes, room for the timetable when it was worked out. It was important to do this to focus my mind on the group.

By this time our new team of seven teachers were meeting informally whenever possible. Most of us had worked together before in the same team, two of us were new to the team. We spent some time discussing the place of mathematics in team work. In our last team maths had been completely separate from the rest of team work and had been taught by only one of us, the team mathematician. This time round we all wanted to share in the maths teaching in one way or another. Then we could begin to explore the relationships between maths and other team work. This time, too, we'd asked to have a scientist working in our team so that we could begin to introduce more scientific activities into the team work. I was glad that science would no longer be a wholly specialised activity outside the team framework.

During the summer holidays I began to collect material and work out my ideas for the beginning of the year. By the end of term it had been clear that none of us felt the need to start the new year off with a grand, common theme – something like The Family with which we had begun our last team's work. We each had our own ideas about how we would start the term off in our own groups. We swopped ideas informally but there was no master plan. Some of my new students had asked for particular things – material for a project they were thinking of doing, a nursery school where they could work, a certain book or type of book. I got together a book on UFOs, material for tapestry-making, ghost stories, *The Life of a Robin* by David Lack. I read through once more all the books in the Penguin English Project series. I arranged a link between the team and a home for mentally handicapped children at Glenfield. At the very end of the holidays I wrote out an 'emergency banda' made up of suggestions for writing for students to try during the first few days, mostly autobiographical in theme.

I came into school three days before the start of term. I find this very important personally, although I do little of worth. I wander round, polish the tables, arrange the tables, rearrange the tables, think in sociometric terms about the tables. I clutter the noticeboards and walls with things and wish that I had more aesthetic sense. I made a decision to risk all from the beginning this year and brought in plants and various objects, hoping nothing got broken or spoiled (nothing has).

It's important to start work as soon as the new students arrive but not simply to impose it – which is difficult when you don't really know the students. Various departments had laid on demonstrations or talks about the kinds of activities they offered, but they didn't seem to be very successful. I felt a bit apologetic and thought things were flagging almost immediately. I got angry with several teachers for not planning their sessions well enough, or so I thought. But the students didn't seem to mind as much as I did. They quite like to chat and circle around each other. By the second day I relaxed more and concentrated on talking individually to students in my group. I didn't leave my area at all.

This is what Phil wrote at the end of his first day:

'I saw new faces as soon as I walked into the pod. Some look friendly and some don't look friendly. I'll have to make friends with them sooner or later. The school is very big and I'll be glad when I know my way around. Countesthorpe is a different school entirely from my last. The teachers seem more friendly and there is much more better things to do. The classes, or pods as they are called here, are a lot more open and don't seal you in like the old fashioned classes at my last school did.'

We talked about this and about his timetable. On the basis of chats with his teachers at the other school, chats with me, and what he had heard from specialists here he chose the following subjects to study (in addition to what he would be studying in team time which would include maths, English, social studies and a variety of other things): art, visual communication, music, control technology, chemistry, PE and games. He had changed his mind about German after talking it over with his parents. He was especially excited by the idea of control technology because of the construction involved, music because of the possibility of using the organ and synthesiser, and visual communication because of a conversation with the person who was going to teach it who had talked about the possibilities of photography. Later he dropped PE and games and said he would play five-a-side 'during team time if he felt the urge'. He also added typing at my suggestion. Here, then, is his present timetable:

	Monday	Tuesday	Wednesday	Thursday	Friday
1	Art	Maths	Music	Team	Maths
2	Chem.	Team	Typing	Team	Team
3	Team	Vis. Comm.	Chem.	Team	C. Tech.
4	Team	Typing	C. Tech.	Team	Team

Each week he uses one of his team lessons to do some extra maths, normally Friday 2. I work with him on Monday afternoon, Tuesday morning all day Thursday, and Friday morning. He is alone on Friday 4. It is an untypical timetable because of the Thursday when he works in the team area all day. But he says he enjoys planning that day most of all. I usually choose then to introduce something new, or at least to have something new handy. We also talk fairly formally then about the progress of all his work, in team and out. I still need to make quasi-formal arrangements to talk with him as he will not initiate a conversation. As soon as I speak though, he rattles on about his work, fishing, astronomy, the piano accordion.

At the start of term I'd suggested to Phil that he kept a journal. This is how he described his school life after two weeks.

'I have been at this school now for two weeks and now I have settled in and doing subjects I like to do and enjoy. Once you get to know the other students they are friendly towards you. When you get down to hard work, time seems to pass a lot quicker, but the first week we were just working out timetables and going to the different classes to see what the different subjects were like and so time seemed to drift slowly by! I like it at this school, you learn things at your own pace and not like at my last school where for example in maths you go through different subjects in that category like an express train so you don't gather much knowledge.'

Phil has been at the school for six weeks now. He does not work quickly, but he sometimes takes work home to finish if it interests him or ideas are fresh in his mind. Sometimes I encourage him to do this, but more often he decides himself and tells me. His journal is no more. His first story was called *Life or Gold*, about explorers being eaten by ants. This was in response to my reading two equally horrifying short stories to the whole class. We talked about his story and I suggested that the theme would make a good poem. He agreed and wrote one quite quickly. It was a rhyming ballad and very fine. We talked about poetry in general. In the process he altered the rhythm of one of the verses in his poem. He insists that poetry must rhyme. I said it needn't and gave him some poems written by students, that don't rhyme. The only one that impressed him at all was one that got in by accident almost, with an insistent rhythm and very regular rhymes. He copied it into his exercise book, he thought it was so good. I questioned him about his reading. We chose *The Naked Sun* by Isaac Asimov. He has just finished it and is now going on to read an Evelyn Waugh novel he found in my box. From discussion about what makes a good book has emerged his own novel, *Invasion*, a science fiction story which promises to go on for several chapters. The subject is time travel and I have helped with technique while feverishly reading up about relativity. He tries to explain the scientific theories behind the plot to me. As yet the novel is in a rough state, but he shows me every page. He sometimes works in the library at this. He discovered the *Thesaurus* one day by chance while writing his novel there and changed the word 'shouted' to 'bawled'. Now he uses it regularly with great excitement. His other written work, apart from the now defunct journal, includes a piece about his friend's grandpa, written after I had read a small group some descriptive pieces, and the beginning of a short piece called 'The Book of the Dead' written after reading the ballad 'The Griesly Wife'.

During the second week of term Phil told me that he would do some work in astronomy after explaining about his telescope and how it worked. I was a bit worried that he felt he had to 'do a project'. This doesn't seem to be the case though, as he is very interested to learn about nebulas and galaxies, partly in order to make his science fiction writing more convincing. Out of our conversations about astronomy we are now starting some historical work on the 'great figures' like Galileo and Copernicus.

I soon found that we were both getting out of our depth in our struggle to understand relativity, despite a lot of reading and discussion. It was time to bring in outside help. I had already mentioned it to a sixth former studying physics and one morning we were given a lecture on the subject during team time. We felt that things were slightly clearer then but we still need more guidance. Luckily a student teacher working in the team at the time was the expert we were looking for and he plans to work quite closely with Phil and me on this topic.

Other work that Phil has got involved in so far this term includes a survey of the birds in Countesthorpe which a friend in his class has started. I hoped that he might be interested in working around the theme of old age after I had read the piece about his friend's grandpa. He thought about it for a week but decided that he wasn't really interested. I was quite sorry about that. Then there's maths. Although I work quite closely with a few of my students on their maths work, Phil is taught almost exclusively by the maths specialist. That's the way he prefers it at the moment and I am happy to leave it like this as long as both he and our maths specialist are satisfied with the way things are going.

Phil's work has begun well. My main regret, looking back over the past six weeks, is that I haven't managed to interest him yet in some of the things that excite me most – like local history, or child development, or the kind of work that involves students in experience outside school. There are other students in my group who are already involved in one or other of these things but so far Phil has not chosen to be. As I continue to work with him one of my aims will be to try and convince him that these things are worth studying too.'

We have been working in teams now for three and a half years, long enough to recognise their value, short enough to know how far we are from making the most of the opportunities they present us. In order to define that opportunity we would return to a proposal put forward by David Hawkins in *Forum* in Autumn 1973. He wrote as follows:

'As many kinds of subject matter are now organised, it is not obvious nor easily possible to transform the teaching of them to a more self-directed and informal style of work in schools. Under these circumstances we are rather likely to fall back into the old polarities. By one party the tradition of the formal course will continue to be seen as for the most part a dreary, ineffective and superficial 'coverage' of subject matter on its way to ossification. By the other party the advocacy of resource-based learning will be seen as a denigration of both rigour and discipline in the mastery of subject matter. What I hope is that this old issue be buried and that we address, instead, the question as to *how* wider ranges of subject matter, of that stuff alluded to in curricula and syllabi, can be revived and reconstituted and extended so as to make it more diversely accessible and appealing to growing minds, more interwoven in the texture of a rich school environment.'

We are rash enough to think that in our teams we are beginning to create the kind of context in which the questions which David Hawkins asks can be fruitfully investigated and even, maybe, answered. That is how we would want to define our opportunity.

5

Discipline

An argument for appropriateness

JOHN WATTS

In an article entitled 'Tell Me What to Do', (published in Discipline
in Schools, *edited by Barry Turner, Ward Lock Educational, 1973) the
editor of this volume argued that former styles of teaching and learning
had forms of discipline that may have been appropriate to them then,
but which would be inappropriate to the changed styles that we have,
for carefully argued reasons, set out to employ today.*

*It is felt that the article is too long to reprint here, but the following
quotation may serve to relate the statement on the development of our
teams, and the various contributions on aspects of curriculum.*

When a parent comes to me and says, 'What my boy needs is more discipline', I think I know what is meant. It means he should be told more
authoritatively by his teachers what 'we' want him to do, but what he does
not want to do, and then punished by enforced pain or inconvenience if
he does not do it. In that way he will learn that life is more comfortable
when conforming and, unless he is very stubborn, he will conform, submit,
obey. This parent makes it sound very simple. All we need to do is to assert
the authority vested in us as schoolmasters and literally master our pupils;
if we fail to do that then we are not worthy of our title and are a right
soft lot into the bargain.

This worries me. It worries me because it all takes for granted a style
of teaching and learning that may have had relevance in some other time
and place, but no longer seems applicable today; it worries me because
that phrase 'what we want' assumes a uniform code of values, which
today, for better or for worse, we do not have; and it worries me because
it renders discipline into something discrete and detached from learning,
a prerequisite to study, rather than something subtly interfused with it
and taking it, colour from it.

I want to argue that discipline, far from being a general condition
registered only in quantity, takes its form from the nature of the work
in hand, determining the kind of relationship arising between teacher

and student. If this is so, then we must start with curriculum and the sort of learning that we want to take place. After that we must ask what is the *appropriate* discipline. For all too often what that parent's boy needs is not more discipline, but a more appropriate discipline. It is not so much a question of getting him to behave before he can learn anything, as one of what kind of behaviour will enable him to learn within the aims of the curriculum.

6

Writing in the Humanities

PAT D'ARCY taught English at Countesthorpe from the time of its opening. She was a project officer with the Schools Council, University of London Institute of Education project: Writing Across the Curriculum. She was co-author of Writing and Learning Across the Curriculum *(Ward Lock Educational, 1975), and she is author of* Reading for Meaning *(Hutchinson Education, 1973). Mrs D'Arcy is currently chairman of the National Association for the Teaching of English, and is head of the English department in a comprehensive school.*

The pamphlet Keeping Options Open *was published in 1974 by the Writing Across the Curriculum project. It was concerned with writing in the humanities, focusing on examples of school-students' writing upon the effects of first-hand experience and their freedom to present their ideas in their own ways. There is insufficient space to relate the examples and Mrs D'Arcy's commentary to the broader theoretical findings of the project, but the extracts used, all drawn from students at Countesthorpe, allow her to trace developments in their writing that point towards a mature awareness of the uses of language.*

In this pamphlet* we have collected together some writings from one of the schools with which we have had close contact – Countesthorpe College in Leicestershire. As many readers will already know, the teachers at Countesthorpe had already made far-reaching audience and situation changes which affected the ethos of the whole school quite independently of the Writing project. As a staff they had agreed from the start that their relationship with students should be based on a principle of mutuality and that wherever possible, choice should be built into the curriculum.

We have obtained, from a small group of pupils studying humanities in their fourth and fifth years, writing and comments which we found encouraging for several reasons: they reflect a wider range of writing audience and function than generally appears to be the case in the later stages of secondary schooling; the fact that external examinations were approaching does not seem to have operated respectively. We know, in fact, that the teachers had made a determined effort to keep writing options open instead of cutting them down. Their success is reflected in

* *Keeping Options Open (Schools Council and University of London Institute of Education, 1974).*

the fact that we didn't have to hunt for examples; writing of the kind we quote here was not exceptional. Another heartening indication that writing was regarded fairly widely as an activity that had point and purpose was that many of the students to whom we talked were enthusiastic about what they had written. They saw writing as a genuine form of communication.

JENNY B'S VISITS TO EDITH

One girl chose to make a study of the grandmother of one of her friends as her major project for the community studies course. Edith was senile and had been taken in by her daughter as she was quite incapable of looking after herself any more. Jenny visited Edith regularly (they lived on the same council estate) from September 1973 to February 1974 when the old lady was taken ill and died in hospital. She wrote down what Edith said verbatim, so her diary of these visits, extracts from which are given below, is another kind of first-hand writing which makes interesting reading for a more public audience than just the teacher.

18.9.73   Persons present: Edith, Cynthia, Penny, Shirley and me.
Edith is sitting on the sofa next to Shirley and we're talking about a tall handsome bloke we met at Bailey's last night and saying what a Casanova he was and she's saying: 'Yes, he looks that way, he looks like him'. Shirley's just asked her to tell me her life story but she says she don't know how to do it.
She's now rumbleing on . . . 'Oh dear. Arn't you very well, oh, I'm glad you're well'. She's now screwing her face up and looking at her hands. 'One, two, three, four.'
She's now looking at me. 'It's nice, I like it. No, it's all right dear, thank you very much, bless you. Yes. Yes. My word isn't he quick,' She's scratching at her skirt again and Shirley's just told her to stop it so she says 'I see well they're big you see.'
She's just pulled her jumper up to make it look like she's got a big chest, she says 'I like to make a laugh' its nice cos we're all laughing at her.
She's scratching again and she says 'I've only had one, I don't know where it came from'.
She's just sitting and smiling now, hang on, she's laughing now because Shirley told her that she looks like something out of Psycho.
Shirley's just pulled her nose so she said 'ow, I've only got one nose. I'll have to buy lots of them, thank you very much, gentlemen'.
Everyone's getting fed up of her now so they've told her to shut up. It won't last long though.
1st November
She's walking around the room fiddling with everything. I'll just ask

her what she's doing. 'I've got some to send tomorrow for Americans. Yours was a good, wasn't it Cynthia?' She's just said to Marie 'Can I turn this telly back so it will be another time?' Marie said 'Yes if you want.' 'Oh thank you very much, I'll go and fetch one.'

I'm just going to show her a photograph of herself. She's showing it to me and saying 'It's me, you wouldn't believe it, that's a good one, I don't look fat there'. She's blowing her cheeks out. 'There I am again, you get sick to death of them, thank you very much dear, thank you.'

25th December

The first thing I'll say to Edith is 'Merry Christmas'. She's just smiling at me. I'll tell her I've got a Christmas present for her and give it to her. 'Thank you dear, mm, yes, mm.' She's put it back on her knee. With a bit of help she finally opens it and says 'Thank you. Oh it's a nice one isn't it, yes, yes it is' and she put it on her knee again. It's a pity she doesn't understand Christmas, I don't think she really realises her son is here even. Poor thing, still at least she's not spending it alone like many old people will.

26th January

I went round and got the shock of my life. Edith is in hospital. Cynth called the doctor this morning and he sent for an ambulance to take her in hospital because she's got a fractured hip.

29th January

The operation has been cancelled because Edith isn't strong enough. She's got a drip in her, but she looks a lot better. She's more talkative. I'll ask her if she's alright. 'Yes thank you. I'm a lot better. I'm fine. Are you dear?' I'm okay, it's her I'm worried about. She looks very tired I'll ask her if she is. 'Yes, just a little, dear'. She's chattering away to herself and I'm very glad for a change. I can't quite make out everything she's saying because she's still not got her bottom teeth in. She's trying to get her hand out of the covers and she's touching my face now and saying how lovely I am. That's really nice. She's took hold of my hand and I feel really upset, my eyes keep watering. I'll have to say goodbye now. 'Yes dear, goodbye and thank you dear, yes, thank you.'

17th February

Today Edith passed away as far as I know in her sleep. I was very upset when I heard and I couldn't stop crying and thinking about her, even though it probably was for the best.

21st February

Today was Edith's funeral. Edith's two sons, Cynth, Penny and I went in the funeral car and although it was quiet and sad, it was a beautiful funeral with lots of gorgeous flowers. I couldn't believe she was in the coffin.

Why write? It's sometimes difficult to give a good reason when talking or doing or reading would have achieved what is to be learnt just as well, perhaps better. But here, unless Jenny had written down exactly what Edith said and did, she would never have been able to convey so poignantly the old lady's personality – and her plight. Her recorded visits are conveyed sympathetically rather than sentimentally and again the function of the writing is many-faceted. It is partly to inform and in the sense that it records what happens we could classify it as transactional writing. But in so far as the writing is also a vehicle for Jenny's own responses ('I'd love to know what she's thinking about . . . I feel really upset, my eyes keep watering . . . It's a pity she doesn't understand Christmas, I don't think she really realises that her son is here even') the writing is expressive – moving overall perhaps towards the poetic as Edith emerges Ophelia-like from the words on the page.

INTERVIEWING PEOPLE

Edith was really too senile to be 'interviewed' by Jenny as her mind wandered too unpredictably from one passing thought to another. Our next two pieces are both based on situations in which people outside the school were asked for their views. For Steve (fourth year) it was the first time that he had based any project work on his own observations. He comments on his work about 'The Students' Demo' as follows:

> A piece of work like this made a pleasant change for me as it was the first time I have ever done anything from first hand information. I was actually at the Demo and interviewed people instead of reading about it afterwards. I would like to do more of my work in this way . . . I find work of this kind by far the most interesting that I have ever done and feel that it is of more value for these reasons : It helps me with talking to people if I interview them for school work and I will always have to talk to people other than those who I know. If I can go to a protest and then write about it then I can go from there and decide what else I want to know about it. It is like having a video-tape of the protest – I have all I want to know (hopefully) on paper and ready for use whenever I want it.

This capacity of written language to capture impressions, and in that sense to hold the options open for further reference and possible modifications later on, was also mentioned by Susan :

> I think it helps to write things down because you can look back and you can remember better from that because if you don't write it down you forget your first impressions of places . . . When you go somewhere the first time it's nice after a few times to look back and find –

compare your first impressions with the one you've got at the moment
. . . Then you can do another piece of work comparing the two.

Interviewing people to discover what their opinions are about a particular
subject is a kind of halfway stage between relying entirely on one's own
experience and using books. For Steve it provided him with a number of
different angles on the students' demo.

In our interviewing we got three main opinions: these are . . .

(1) It's a complete waste of my time and yours.
  (This came from the two elderly women)
(2) It's worth trying but I don't think you will get anywhere.
  (This came from one of the students)
(3) Yes it is worth it and I think they will succeed.
  (This came from one of the students and the policeman)

For Alison, who chose to do her community studies project on adoption,
interviewing two friends of the family who had themselves adopted two
children gave her a more immediate contact with the adoptive situation
(from the parents' point of view) than simply reading about it could have
done, and her sense that she is drawing on real experience is reflected in the
writing.

– After being accepted they had a wait of fourteen months before anything further happened. They had asked for a little boy but Jean said
that if she was adopting now she wouldn't make that stipulation. For
the first six months after being accepted Jean said that she was really
keyed up and ready to receive the baby, but as time went by this faded
a little, as Martin said, 'You can't stay pregnant forever!' so when the
letter came saying that there was a six week old baby waiting to be
adopted it was a mad rush to get everything ready.
– Martin and Jean had a great deal of support from their close rela-
tives who were all delighted that they were going to adopt and some
of their closest friends were already adoptive parents.
– 'The only odd comments we got were from people who were near
strangers. I remember one distant relative of Martin's before we actually adopted David, but after we had started telling people. He came up
to us and said "I think that's a wonderful thing you are going to do!
It's very Christian of you" as if we were going to take a poor ragged
orphan into our home, when all the time we were desperate to have a
child.'
– We talked a bit about matching and Martin and Jean thought that
on the whole it was better if the two sets of parents' intelligence was

matched so that intelligent adoptive parents with more to offer an intelligent child would have at least as much chance of having a bright child as if he was born to them.

– Finally Jean told me about the most difficult stage of the adoption, 'it was when we were childless. The attitudes we met then were far more hurtful than any we've met since we adopted. It's absolutely amazing how people assume that you are childless by choice. We may have had some tactful friends who never mention it but the number of people who said quite openly 'Well when are you going to have a family then?' or 'Its all very well for you having holidays abroad, you won't be able to do that when you've got a family' things like that at that stage when we were desperately wanting children were very hurtful and at that stage you don't particularly want to say to people that you are trying to have a family and can't. It's very private.'

Anecdote, discussion, honest comments from someone who knows from experience what it's like – it gives a sense of focus to Alison's writing which a more generalised commentary often lacks. She ends her account of the interview with the footnote 'Martin and Jean were extremely interesting to talk to and I learned a great deal from them'. Clearly the chance to discuss what it's like to adopt children had been a valuable experience. Did the writing add anything? It is difficult to be categorical about this – but if Susan's remarks and Steve's are anything to go by ('It's like having a video-tape . . . because if you don't write it down you forget your first impressions . . .'), the act of writing it down may have helped to fix what was said in Alison's mind, thus helping her also to be more aware of her attitudes to it. Writing gives a shape which doesn't blur at the edges with the passing of time.

A RANGE OF WRITING OPPORTUNITIES

The writings that have been quoted so far have tended to be in the expressive function because we wanted to show how the flexibility of such a close-to-thought, close-to-talk writing can be as appropriate and helpful to older pupils as it can to 7- or 8-year-olds. Adolescents like comfortable clothes for playing and working in too – and expressive writing is not dissimilar to this kind of gear in the ease of movement it allows.

The original Writing Research team have suggested that expressive writing is the matrix out of which the various forms of transactional and poetic writings grow: transactional on the one hand as a tool for *participating* in one way or another in the world's affairs, poetic on the other hand as a means of *contemplating* past experiences and of sharing our memories and reflections with a wider audience.

Susan's writing about her first visit to a geriatric hospital is a real mixture of these two stances – at one moment she is recollecting what happened and standing back to contemplate her feelings retrospectively, at other points in the writing she is speculating about what might happen in the future – almost planning in advance : 'I know that it is difficult to cope with old people and lift them around when you have got families of your own to deal with but I'd rather my parents died at home together or at least in familiar personal surroundings . . . '

This movement between spectator and participant roles is characteristic of writing which is 'expressive', but in some of the other pieces that we have quoted we can see how the *trend* of the writing is moving away from the expressive either towards a more informational or decision-making function or towards a more contemplative one. Steve's writing about the student's demo would illustrate the former and Jenny B's writing about Edith, the latter.

There were examples in the writing of all the students whose work we have used of pieces that could be classified as dominantly transactional or dominantly poetic. In other words, they were all capable of spreading out across the whole range of writing functions in work of their own choice. Again, the study of a project appeared to encourage this kind of diversity in so far as different writing functions helped the writer to explore the topic from different angles. Steve, for instance, who disliked what he called 'creative writing' (about 'Water and Wind' . . .) had this to say about the relevance of imaginative writing to project work :

I write stories occasionally – yeh, it does appeal to me writing stories and writing creative things does – if – so long as I can pick what I want to do – you know – if I feel like writing a story . . . it tends to be to illustrate what, er, my factual work's in – say if I did, er, Vietnam – a story might be about some Vietnamese child or other whose parents had been killed in warfare or something like that. . . . I think it can be as helpful as having the factual thing. You know, one needs the other sort of thing, because I can write as much as I like about this factual thing in Vietnam – what the Americans are using, and what it does to your skin if it's napalm or – and the dates and things, but it still doesn't really explain what life's like in Vietnam – it just gives people a load of facts, a bit like having a computer.

In his own words Steve is explaining how writing in the poetic function is concerned to explore feelings. What he doesn't mention, however, is the other central characteristic of this function – its *presentation* of such feelings in an increasingly formalised fashion as a construct – a work of art which can be offered to the reader partly for him to contemplate and partly for pleasure. Here is an example, a poem written by Jenny B in a context very different from her visits to Edith :

Our Love Tree

We'd meet at our love tree everyday
And we'd hold hands and talk,
And sometimes, if we were in the mood
We'd go for a little walk.
Those were happy days I remember
In the beautiful days of summer
From June to September.
You bought a penknife one day
And inscribed our names on the tree,
I inscribed I loved you
And you inscribed you loved me.
We were so happy together
With the birds singing
And the lovely weather.
But with less holding hands and talking
We knew it wouldn't last,
So we kissed our love tree goodbye
And left it in the past.
Memories flow back
When I walk by our love tree
As it turns black.

By contrast, as an example of writing which is clearly transactional, here is a further piece from Alison's study on 'Adoptability' to show how, sometimes, generalised classificatory writing can serve an entirely appropriate writing function, especially when the student is basing what he or she writes on material already in print.

Adoptability

Perhaps the most difficult decision to be made directly concerning the child in adoption is whether or not he should be placed for adoption. It is generally agreed that for most children an adoptive home is better than a foster child's home, but it is not always as cut and dried as that. When possible the natural parents are encouraged to keep their child but the fact that the child has been taken into care in the first place indicates some sort of neglect or incapacity on the part of the parents and how does one decide at what point the neglect and rejection of the parents becomes such that it is no longer possible for the child to return home?

There are cases of children who have spent years in care and whose parents rarely or never visit but who still maintain that one day they are going to take the child back. How can it be decided whether or not there really is a parental tie between the child and his parents?

These are just two of the immensely difficult questions that the adoption worker has to answer when deciding whether or not a child should be placed for adoption. There are basically three reasons why many deprived children are not considered adoptable:

(a) it is thought that the natural parents should retain their responsibilities

(b) on the grounds of the child's health, hereditary background or emotional problems it is felt that adoption is too great a risk

(c) the agency does not think that a suitable home can be found.

The subject of parental rights and responsibilities is one that a lot of people feel strongly about. Parents should be held responsible for their children's welfare is the general opinion and probably the right one. . . .

This is highly competent transactional writing. Alison's own voice has receded into the background – the language is cool, the tone neutral. Because it is both competent and informative the audience for whom the writing is fully meaningful is public rather than personal – there is no need to rely on any inside knowledge of either the writer or the situation in which she is writing for it to be fully understood. To be able to write impersonally and analytically is certainly one of the increasing number of choices that the developing writer should be able to make.

Are pupils likely to write more – and more discriminatingly – if the range of writing audience and writing function is held open rather than closed down as they move up the secondary school? It is difficult to answer this question at all categorically, especially as the general pattern seems to be towards narrowing the range in the face of external examinations. Nevertheless the question remains: is a preponderance of classificatory transactional writing produced for a teacher who is regarded predominantly in an examiner/assessor role either educationally necessary or desirable? For the students whose written work we have used in this pamphlet, the reverse appears to be the case. They have demonstrated that when it is appropriate they can take up such informational writing adequately, but in addition they have also taken up other options – to write expressively, thoughtfully, sometimes tentatively about topics which genuinely concerned them. They have shown that it is possible to write for an unknown public audience. They have also, by their own account, engaged in using written language in the process of self-discovery, putting down their thoughts into words that can be read and returned to, as a valuable aid to learning.

Individualised learning has been the key to mixed-ability groupings and the whole system of personal-contract timetabling at Countesthorpe. The techniques of this approach are not known all that widely yet. Students are learning increasingly from resources made available to them through the school, though not necessarily *in* the school. The material resources are varied and teachers need to be skilful in producing, storing and retrieving them. Where expertise has been developed, it needs to be shared.

The science teachers at Countesthorpe have been in the forefront of such developments. Eric Green, head of physical sciences, organised a national conference at the College in 1973 from which grew ILIS (Independent Learning in Science.) He is editor of *Towards Independent Learning in Science* (Hart-Davis, 1975).

When teachers first introduce individualised learning, they tend to rely heavily on their own home-produced worksheets. Because students will at first ask 'What are we meant to do?', the worksheets tend to be prescriptive. They may differ from textbooks only in being more carefully tailored to know groups of students, and, it must be said, often less attractively presented. With experience we have come to rely less and less on worksheets, more on varied resources, made available to students as they move along their individual paths of study.

7

Individualised Learning in Science, and Worksheets

My Changing Attitudes Towards Them

JEFF SHAPLAND

JEFF SHAPLAND has had charge of chemistry since Countesthorpe opened. He has served as chairman of standing committee and was one of the first two teachers elected by staff to attend governors' meetings.

In the following two papers by Jeff Shapland we see the practical working of a chemistry teacher and the development of that practice in the light of experience. In particular, Jeff Shapland explains his changed view of the part played by worksheets.

The first article appeared in New Movements in the Study and Teaching of Chemistry, *edited by Dr D. J. Daniels (Maurice Temple Smith, 1975). The second appeared in a periodical publication of the project Writing Across the Curriculum in January 1975, entitled* Writing in Science in Schools.

The group of boys and girls near the door are studying for O level or CSE following a Nuffield-based course. They work mainly from printed worksheets which contain instructions for experiments, theoretical ideas, background information, problems and references to reading books, and so on. Each section of work – about six to ten worksheets – ends with a test, and to cover an O level course they tend to do about twelve sections of work. In fact those doing the energy topic have almost completed the O level work in just over one year. They could start advanced work soon or study something which particularly interests them. Near the window is a group of boys who are much less able and much less interested in chemistry, or any science. I've persuaded them to work from the booklet on fuels which I wrote some time ago. This includes a wider range of things to do such as a crossword, simulation exercise, project ideas, as well as experimental work. The bench over there contains a mixture of people : the two on the end are doing some project work on photography which arises out of work they were doing in another part of the school. The girls opposite them are trying to make dyes from plant material, and will probably go on to do the section of work on fibres. Next to them is a group who are working on the rates of reaction section. They have become much more confident at setting up their own experiments although they still need a lot of help. The group on the last bench includes three boys from the lower sixth. Two of them are starting chemistry for the first time and one took a CSE last year and wants to take O level this year. The two working at the fume cupboard are finishing an experiment they started in this morning's A level class.

That is a brief description of the type of independent learning system operated by the author at Countesthorpe College for the past four years. It seems that there are many definitions and interpretations of the term 'independent learning' although they undoubtedly all have some features in common. For example, Reid and Booth define three categories of independent learning: short-term independent learning which takes place within one lesson: medium-term independent learning, a topic-by-topic approach, which might last three or four weeks; and long-term independent learning which might last for a two-year course or longer. They define independent learning as 'any situation where a group of pupils are working at their own pace' (Reid and Booth, 1974). This categorisation is undoubtedly a useful one, although it is important to realise that there are other factors, apart from length of time, which can distinguish independent learning systems. I believe that student choice of material to be studied is an important factor in independent learning, and therefore see little use for the first category. Current educational thinking suggests that at least some degree of self-regulation is essential to all learning, and many would go farther than that. I see independent learning as a system which allows individuals and groups within a class to learn different things in different ways at their own pace. It follows that pupils must be allowed as much choice as possible over the work they do, as well as being allowed to do it at a rate, and in a manner, appropriate to themselves. Of course they will not be left to their own devices, and much of this chapter will be devoted to exploring the laboratory arrangements and teacher role needed to enable this to happen.

SOME ADVANTAGES OF INDEPENDENT LEARNING

The Nuffield Science Teaching project, which has brought about so many changes in science teaching in Britain, quoted the Chinese proverb: 'I hear and I forget. I see and I remember. I do and I understand.' It is because independent learning enables pupils to do things for themselves, and therefore to learn more effectively, that it is most valuable as a learning method in chemistry and other subjects. Students are not only enabled to carry out experiments at their own speed, but to repeat them as many times as they wish in order to make them work, or to increase their understanding. The experiments may well suggest other lines of inquiry tangential to the direction in which pupils are moving, and there is no reason why these should not be followed up, with the teacher's help and guidance. Students sometimes have their own ideas for experiments and, as most teachers know, they can learn most when they are highly motivated in this way. Some students may want to start a course at different times from others: perhaps they realise that they made a wrong option choice: they may have been ill for some time; or have moved from another area with a different chemistry background; all these can be allowed to work from their own position. Sometimes students do not need to follow a complete course, but only to do some chemistry because they need it for a career or to back up other studies.

Under this scheme students not only learn chemistry, they have to learn to take responsibility for, and to organise, their own learning. The teacher is freed from the role of class organiser and direct source of information, to become a helper, an encourager, and to relate more directly to all students in the class. This change in the role of the teacher is very important and will be discussed at length later.

It often seems that independent learning is so closely related to teaching mixed-ability groups that it has no other *raison d'être*, but although the author believes that mixed-ability groups are desirable, it can be seen from the above independent learning is an important development in any learning situation. However it is undoubtedly true that it is an essential method for operating mixed-ability groups, and that is where most interest lies.

THE ROLE OF THE TEACHER

It is essential in independent learning schemes, as in any other, that the teacher is fully involved in the learning processes. Anyone who thinks that it is only necessary to have the right laboratory organisation and a set of perfect worksheets in order to be able to sit back while the students teach themselves is badly mistaken. Some would have us believe that once good materials are prepared and the laboratories suitably organised non-science teachers could be used to relieve the shortage of science teachers. This is certainly not so, although a well-organised system can be of great help to an inexperienced teacher. As in any system, the teacher's first task is to decide how the learning will take place and to organise the laboratory and materials so that it can do so.

There is a wide variety of written resource material which can be made available, and it is the teacher's job to be familiar with the materials, either through having written them himself, or by working through them. The laboratory must be organised in such a way that apparatus, chemicals, written resources and little things like pins, string, sellotape and filter paper are readily available to students, aspects of safety and security being borne in mind.

If this is not done there is a real danger that the teacher will spend most of the lesson finding things so that the pupils can do their practical work. Even in the best-run laboratories things can 'go missing', or the situation might arise where an experiment needs materials which are not normally available. If this happens it is important that the materials should be added to those normally kept in the laboratory as soon as possible, otherwise students will begin to lose confidence that the things they need are available. This lack of confidence can be seen most clearly in students who have only recently joined the school. In my experience it takes four to six weeks, after a careful introduction, before students are confident that most of the things they require are to hand. Of course there are always the attention-seekers, who ask for something they know is there, or the lazy ones who hope the teacher will get it for them!

On entering a class-teaching it is usually fairly clear who the teacher is; most things centre upon him and visitors are obvious. In an independent learning situation, however, the teacher is much less obvious, although his role is just as important. He or she will be moving from group to group in the laboratory: sometimes helping to do an experiment, sometimes helping to solve problems, encouraging some, motivating others or quietening a noisy group. He must know what each group or individual is doing and assess their ability so as to be able to guide them. A difficult decision is when to intervene in a group's work. If the members are struggling with a problem, should we tell them the answer in order to speed them along, or give them a hint and let them struggle a little longer? It is no use waiting until students ask for help, as some never will. Even if we ask 'Are you getting on all right?' the answer is likely to be more often 'Yes' than 'No'. No one likes to admit that they cannot understand, and some prefer a 'quiet life' at any cost. I try to sit with each group, or individual, for some part of each lesson, sometimes intervening, sometimes just observing.

It is of the utmost importance that written work does not dominate. We shall see later some ways of avoiding this situation when preparing materials, but one way is to vary the approach so that students feel that the teacher is just as much in control as in a class-teaching situation. Indeed we would hope that they would feel even more in touch with the teacher, and he with them. Whole-group activities such as stimulus lectures, films or discussions, are valuable in generating a feeling of group identity and in focusing attention on some aspect of the work. These occasions may be with a whole class or with a group within a class. The latter is easier in some form of team teaching.

As well as knowing what the students are doing, the teacher must assess their progress and performance. In mixed-ability groups this is particularly difficult because of the variety of work being undertaken. The author uses an extended register to record what work each student is doing, or has done each lesson. This has the advantage that the progress of groups can be assessed quickly so that other materials can be introduced for some students. It also shows up any students who are not being seen regularly by the teacher, as there will be blanks against their names. There is great advantage too in organising the work into short units or modules, with test materials at the end of each unit, so that the student has to perform tests at intervals of, say, not more than a month; and at this point the work can be closely marked by the teacher, and any revision processes thought necessary undertaken. In general it is desirable to correct as much work as possible during the lesson so that the student can participate in the process. In a mixed-ability situation it is essential to mark according to the standard expected from individual students. If this is not done there is a real risk of the less able becoming depressed at their slower progress, and the more able failing to be fully stretched because they consider themselves so far ahead. It is essential for pupils to be able to assess their own progress, with the teacher's help, both for themselves, and with regard to the demands of external examinations.

It should be clear from the above that independent learning makes possible, and almost demands, a much closer interaction between students and teacher than is normally the case. Teachers have come down from their pedestals and have to leave the safety of the demonstration bench to sit alongside students and join in the learning process. They are more likely to be seen to have 'forgotten' or to have to admit 'I don't know, let's go and look it up', than when they were able to hide behind their lesson-preparation notes. In return they can look forward to getting to know their students more thoroughly, to discovering more about their learning difficulties than they probably would in class-teaching, and to working with groups of students who are more likely to be enjoying the work they do. Professor Elton, who is probably one of the few people in Britain to use independent learning methods in university science teaching, says of his experience 'I've learned more in one year about the interactions that the students have with what they study than in the previous twenty-five. It's been a completely new dimension of awareness of the teaching and learning process . . .' (Sherwood, 1973). The conclusions of many science teachers who operate independent learning are similar.

WRITTEN RESOURCES

The most commonly used paper resource for independent learning in science is the worksheet. In its simplest form this might consist of a list of apparatus and chemicals needed for an experiment, instructions for carrying out the practical work and a diagram of the experimental set-up, followed by help with presentation of the results, calculations and/or questions on the topic with spaces left for the answers to be written on the worksheet.

There are many advantages in using worksheets. Students have constant access to the instructions and are not dependent on the teacher writing them on the board or giving them orally. They can easily check the instructions if they forget them and a good diagram of the apparatus is readily available. Much time is saved by students not having to write up the experiments formally, and thus more time can be spent in answering questions about the experiment and doing calculations. If it is felt desirable for students to learn to write up experiments this can be incorporated as one of the tasks on the worksheets. Students can build up a file of completed worksheets, perhaps interleaved with their own work on file paper. As well as worksheets, theory sheets, project sheets and test sheets can be used. A good example of such a scheme for physics teaching is that used by E. L. Green (Green, 1972). If worksheets are to be successful, they must be well prepared and carefully written.

The following thoughts are based on four years' experience of writing and rewriting worksheets and are offered for those who have little experience in this field. It is important that the writer has a clear objective for the worksheet and that attention is given to layout. It is usually helpful to list the apparatus and chemicals required, and to itemise the steps in the practical work. A decision has to be taken as to whether students should be asked to record their observations on the worksheets during or after the practical work. Think carefully about the amount of room left for the students' comments. Too little space will result in cramped, messy work which may be unintelligible in the future; too much space leaves the worksheet looking blank and can escalate printing costs. If a lot of writing is required for a particular piece of work it is probably a good idea to ask that it be done on file paper, which can be interleaved with the worksheets. Always check for errors and ambiguities, if possible by asking students to read through the materials before printing. Everyone who has written worksheets has probably suffered the time-wasting queries which result from even a small error, and ambiguities can result in students carrying out experiments which were never intended. One of the chief sources of error in this respect seems to arise from the instruction 'Now repeat the experiment but instead of using . . .'. A particular problem in chemistry is how to deal with experiments which must be done by a teacher. Too many 'Your teacher will now show you . . .' instructions result both in an impossible load being placed on the teacher, and often in several disillusioned students. An example of this kind of experiment is reacting the alkali metals with water. Here it is a good idea to give careful instructions on the worksheet so that the student can get all the necessary apparatus assembled, say in the fume cupboard, and then call the teacher, who need only spend a few minutes demonstrating the experiment and leave the student to clear away. At other times it might be necessary to give some details about the results of an experiment with the statement 'you will see this demonstrated as a class experiment during the year'. Avoid lengthy written instructions: many students will not read them and the less able might not be able to do so. Illustrations and good clear diagrams often convey information more clearly and concisely than words. It is usually best to type most of the wording, but variety can be introduced by having some parts in clear legible handwriting, or block capitals, thus making the material seem more personal to the student.

Before leaving the subject of worksheets it is only fair to consider some of their disadvantages. It seems clear from my experience that they are most successful with higher ability students of 14-plus, and those who are particularly well motivated. Below average ability students are usually harder to stimulate by even very well produced worksheets. A continuous 'diet' of worksheets can lead to the feeling on the students' part that the main aim of chemistry is to complete as many worksheets as quickly as possible, and reluctance to accept any suggestion – even if it is written on the worksheet – that they should undertake activities which prevent them completing yet more worksheets. Indeed the worksheets can come between the teacher and the student, thus preventing the very interaction they were designed to generate. A further disadvantage is that worksheets are of limited use in a problem-solving approach. It is difficult to encourage students to plan how to tackle a problem by use of a worksheet.

Finally, there is some concern at the way structured worksheets which demand little more than one-word answers may limit the students' use of language, and this could play a crucial part in the learning process. Those who would like more information on this are referred to the pamphlet *Writing in Science in Schools* (Schools Council and University of London Institute of Education, 1975).

From the foregoing it should be clear that worksheets have a valuable role in independent learning but that there are dangers in their exclusive use. Another resource which has many of the characteristics of the worksheet but which is different in use is the work booklet. The main difference is that students do not write in the work booklets, and since they can be re-used it is usually possible to include more extensive illustration than would be possible or desirable in worksheets. They can be looked upon more as a resources package; the student may not work through all the booklet but pick out the parts relevent to his study. They are particularly useful for wider ranging topics such as detergents, plastics, fuels, and so on and can include more background information and project ideas than worksheets. They are often more acceptable to the less well-motivated who do not see them as part of a large organised system. A development of the work booklet is the heat-sealed card, which can include a wider variety of material, in particular coloured illustrations from magazines. The disadvantage of these is that it is usually only possible to produce one of each and there is a risk of loss. On the other hand the plastic film protects them well so that they can be used for a long time without damage. They are particularly useful for less able students.

For those who have not previously undertaken independent learning, the task of providing enough resources must seem formidable. It is often possible to form teams of teachers to write materials, either within a particular school or at a local teachers' centre. Sometimes it is possible to use other teachers' material in order to start a scheme. The organisation called Independent Learning in Science which has members throughout Britain and abroad was set up to facilitate this sort of exchange.

Apart from the resources mentioned, books, periodicals, 'Jackdaws', films and film loops, videotapes, and so on, can all be used in independent learning. It is my conviction that independent learning works best when a variety of resources for learning are used and the teacher retains a central role.

LABORATORY ORGANISATION

As mentioned earlier, students must be able to locate the materials they need in the laboratory quickly and easily. The organisation of particular laboratories will vary according to the type of work being undertaken, the type of student using it and the financial situation of the school. As an example there follows a description of the author's laboratory, which is now used to teach 14- to 18-year-old students, and which illustrates some of the techniques which have been developed. Solid chemicals are stored on shelves in large jars with numbers painted on the jar and the lid. This makes it easy to check that all the jars are present and that they are in order so that they can easily be found. For the sake of safety only small amounts of materials such as sulphur and iodine are put out, and in these cases the small container is kept inside one of the larger jars (both being numbered). A list of compounds in alphabetical order is used to identify the number of the jar required. Solutions and liquids are treated in a similar fashion and altogether nearly 150 chemicals are made available to students in this way. Despite this it is only very occasionally that chemicals are misused.

Glassware and other pieces of apparatus are stored in drawer units, which have the name of the contents painted on them. Larger pieces of apparatus, such as retort-stands and tripods, are stored in the laboratory so that they can easily be seen by the students. The laboratory system more often than not breaks down because of lack of small things like scissors, thermometers and teat-pipettes. Various methods have been developed to prevent these being lost, accidentally or otherwise. In particular, an easily checkable unit which contains small numbers of things has been devised. Indeed it is worth noting that an independent learning system may well be more economical on apparatus because the more efficient manner in which it is used. We never put out more than three thermometers, or more than six teat-pipettes, and rarely have to supplement these. For some topics we make up units of chemicals and apparatus which are stored in drawer units or small mobile cupboards. These are particularly useful for work in the work booklets used by less able students.

Clearly, technical help is essential in this organisation and the role of the technician is changed from one in which class sets and teacher demonstrations are prepared to one in which a laboratory has to be maintained in working order and new methods constantly sought to ensure its smooth functioning.

CONCLUSION

Independent learning in chemistry allows us to tailor a course of study to a particular student's aptitude and ability. It demands a change in the role of the teacher into one involving closer student/teacher interaction, which should result in improved learning and development on the part of the student.

REFERENCES

E. L. Green (1972), 'Individualised Learning in Physics', *School Service Review*, Vol. 54, No. 187.
D. J. Reid and P. Booth (1974), 'Independent Learning in Science – a review of present progress', *School Science Review*, Vol. 55, No. 192.
Schools Council and London University Institute of Education (1975), joint project 'Writing Across the Curriculum', *Writing in Science in Schools*.
M. Sherwood (1973), 'Educational Innovators', *New Scientist*, 7 June 1973.
For assistance contact Independent Learning in Science, Countesthorpe College, Winchester Road, Countesthorpe, Leicestershire. (Various newsletters and catalogues of resources.)

WORKSHEETS – MY CHANGING ATTITUDES TOWARDS THEM

In retrospect there are two reasons why we chose to use worksheets when Countesthorpe opened in 1970: (a) to enable us to operate mixed-ability groups; (b) to enable students to work at their own pace. Our example was undoubtedly the Nuffield Foundation Resources for Learning project. I can't remember ever doubting that this was the best way to operate. I do so now for several reasons. As regards mixed-ability teaching, I taught previously in a nine-form entry banded comprehensive, but we taught the same content to each band in the first year. So each band did, for instance, the rock salt experiment. So why do we now think that we have to write a worksheet for it just because the pupils are mixed instead of being in bands? If we feel that our approach to the different bands was different, and that this was a necessary part of the learning process, then it is logical that we should have several different varieties of worksheets on 'rock salt' for the different kids. Apart from the fact that this introduces a form of streaming into a mixed-ability situation, we should never be able to cope with the production. I can see no reason why we couldn't carry on the 'rock salt type' activity with first years in mixed-ability groups without worksheets for it.

What about students working at their own speed? Two ways of operating independent learning in mixed-ability groups are: (i) a topic-by-topic approach – what Reid and Booth call short-term independent learning, and (ii) long-term independent learning, where pupils can move as rapidly as they wish. Reid and Booth conclude that long-term independent learning is less likely to be successful, except in highly structured courses (perhaps physics) and that it is rarely operated. So it would seem that many of the hundreds of worksheets being produced at present are probably for use in short-term (or medium-term) independent learning, with all pupils (say) covering the topic of 'energy' or 'water', but with some doing it in greater depth. It would seem to me that in this situation it would not be impossible to operate without highly structured worksheets. Some written material, instructions, stimulating ideas, yes.

But there are other reasons why I became increasingly unhappy about the large-scale use of worksheets. First, because they only cater for the upper ability ranges. The average and below average are rarely stimulated by even the most attractively produced worksheet and many are less than that! Second because, although the use of worksheets frees the teacher from the central role of initiating all the activity, he is often replaced in the pupils' minds by the worksheet. I have seen kids as lost when the worksheets ran out as they used to be when the teacher didn't turn up. And, more important, the worksheets can come between the teacher and pupil, so although the teacher has more time to go to each group there is not a corresponding increase in pupil/teacher interaction. The student is often relating more to the worksheet. When I ask 'What exactly are you doing?' I often get the answer 'This bit here' (and they point to it).

Another worry is how far worksheets can encourage a scientific approach to problems, how far they can encourage a problem-solving approach. In particular, how can 'planning how to tackle a problem' be encouraged if the worksheet goes on to state exactly what must be done to solve it?

And finally, but perhaps most important of all (after the science seminar at Wansfell), I am concerned at the way worksheets limit the students' use of language which could be so crucial in the learning process. If it is true that our first drafts of thinking start in the expressive and that the thrashing out of ideas in expressive language plays a crucial part in understanding, then it is clear that many of the worksheets I have written and many other people's do not (and possibly could not) make provision for this. Nuffield stated the case for pupils' records being personal back in 1966 but we forgot that in our enthusiasm to produce worksheets.

So what now? Can we have a bonfire of all our worksheets, sell the offset litho and banda machines and dismiss our printers? I think not. We need printed materials and for some aspects of our work we may need worksheets. I would favour the following approach. For the first three years we should hope to do without closely structured worksheets on which pupils write. Small booklets of ideas and information may be required and other resources such as heat-sealed cards. (It is interesting that this is the way things have evolved – through feeling rather than rational thought – at Countesthorpe for years 1–3.) In addition I would hope to see the use of written language encouraged positively – especially in imaginative situations. The problem with fourth and fifth years' mixed-ability work, where some are working towards O level/CSE and some do the subject for interest's sake only, is more difficult. In chemistry, I operate long-term independent learning for this age-range but I am only too well aware that those who gain most are the brightest students. They forge ahead, work enthusiastically and intelligently from the printed sheets, and get a good grasp of the subject almost without any help from me. And that is a cause for concern! Within a group of 20–5 fourth/fifth years there will be only about four groups of four working towards exams, and probably only six groups of four overall. I would like to explore the possibility of working with the groups, setting problems to be solved, advising on experiments, discussing results, and guiding them to background reading on a teacher/student basis without the worksheet coming in between.

Independent learning without worksheets – can it be done? If it can, I think the learning situation could be very much improved; the gulf between those who can operate with worksheets and those who can't would be narrowed, and everybody might be able to contribute to the raising and solving of the problems and we might get genuine mixed-ability teaching. I intend to discuss it further with my colleagues with a view to trying it in the near future.

8

Reconstructing Knowledge

An example

MICHAEL ARMSTRONG

MICHAEL ARMSTRONG's reflections upon five years' full-time teaching at Countesthorpe have led him to reconsider the whole process of learning. A fuller exposition of this development awaits publication. Glimpses of it may be had by reading the correspondence with Professor Bantock, pp. 161–82. An introduction may also be had from his article reprinted here from Forum, *Vol. 17, No. 2 (Spring 1975).*

My contention is that the process of education should imply a dynamic relationship between teacher, pupil and task out of which knowledge is reconstructed, for both teacher and pupil, in the light of a shared experience. I want to try to illustrate the relationship and its fruits from my own limited and tentative experience in a Leicestershire upper school.

I think that the relationship in question depends upon a number of preconditions – upon unstreaming for example, upon a re-integration of 'pastoral' care and 'academic' care – and above all upon an acknowledgement of every pupil's capacity for, and need of, autonomy in the pursuit of knowledge. Here I shall focus attention on the experience of learning itself and on the collaborative context in which it thrives.

That context might be defined as the kind which encourages 'conversation'. There is a fascinating paragraph in one of R. S. Peters's essays in which he sets out to define the quality of a conversation.

'Conversation is not structured like a discussion group in terms of one form of thought, or towards the solution of a problem. In a conversation lecturing to others is bad form; so is using the remarks of others as springboards for self-display. The point is to create a common world to which all bring their distinctive contributions. By participating in such a shared experience much is learnt, though no one sets out to teach anyone anything. And one of the things that is learnt is to see the world from the viewpoint of another whose perspective is very different.'

Unfortunately, but not unexpectedly, Peters assumes that 'conversation' is possible only between people who are already 'well-educated'. A large part of the contemporary philosophy of education rests on this mistake. By contrast, my experience of working and talking with children and adolescents suggests that the conversational form, much as Peters describes it, is a characteristic of the most fruitful encounters between teachers and pupils throughout the process of education.

I shall describe one particular episode in my most recent experience which seems to share something of the conversational spirit. Of course by far the greater part of my and my colleagues' work at Countesthorpe is not yet of this kind. Much of it is still heavily didactic, rooted in the scholastic tradition and imprisoned by our own inflexibility of mind.

Carol is a 16-year-old student who lives on a council estate on the outskirts of Leicester. She'd like to work with children eventually and she's hoping to get accepted for an NNEB training course at the end of the year. Towards the end of last term I asked her whether she'd like to spend one day a week this term working in a small village primary school about five miles away. A friend of mine taught there, I knew something of his work and admired and envied it, and I felt the experience would be valuable for Carol. By the time I talked it over with her I already had a good idea of what, in general terms, I hoped she would get out of it – experience of working with children, an opportunity to observe an exceptional teacher, and a chance to acquire, through experience and study, the beginnings of a general understanding of learning and development in young children.

Carol's attitude, I think, was that she would try it and see. 'I was expecting big things' she wrote later; but she was equally certain that she wouldn't stick at it if she found herself bored, frustrated or ignored, as I think she half suspected she might be.

I didn't say much about the school before we first went, only that it was very small, that I'd been there and liked it a lot, and that I thought the teacher she'd be working with was rather exceptional. I warned her not to expect too much to begin with and I asked her to keep a regular diary of each week's visit.

The first visit was quite a shock. Carol found she was far more constrained than she'd imagined. 'First I went to see the boys doing woodwork. I asked a little boy what he was making. He told me he was making a whale and that he was trying to make it smooth with some sandpaper, and that was it, end of conversation. I think he was dying to tell me all about the whale but I just couldn't find the words to say anything to him.'

As she moved from group to group her responses grew more complex. 'I went up to the top end of the room where Mike was reading with a little girl. Then he let me take over. I felt rather strange because things flashed through my head to when I was sitting on a tiny chair reading with a little piece of paper under the line so that you don't lose the line you're reading. It really took me back. I felt rather big, learning her new words, not big-headed but that I was helping somebody to learn something new. After two pages of reading I thought I'd let her read on her own, as she seemed very nervous about it all and soon as I got up from the table she started chatting to her friends. I would have loved to know what she was saying about me.'

Talking and writing about the morning afterwards helped Carol to clarify her feelings and to sharpen her perception but the disappointment of not getting on 'more freely' remained. The following week was worse if only because it was no better. When I came to pick Carol up at the end of the morning she seemed more worried because I was late than interested in what she'd been doing. I talked to her a little about what we might do to help things along and later I made one or two suggestions in her diary but she hadn't had time to read them before the next Friday came. On the way to the village that day she told me should wouldn't go again unless things worked out better. I was mildly worried.

When I came back at the end of the morning, on time this time, she was really excited. All the way back in the car she chatted about what she'd done. I wasn't going to see her again before the following week and asked her to make sure to write everything in her diary before it all slipped her mind. On the Monday she brought me the account that follows.

I didn't fancy going this week at all, over the thought that not one child would talk to us or anything.

Just before we got to the classroom thoughts went through my head that they would all turn round and stare at us again. I wish I knew what they thought of us, I think I'll ask them one day.

Well as I expected they turned round and stared at us as if to say oh no not them again, but! nevertheless my mind didn't listen. I just went straight on in. First I went up to the boys. Well anybody could see they were dying for me to ask what they had got in their miniature garden, so I asked them. Well they had made a garden and planted lots of plants and grass and things like that. Then they had collected lots of insects and things like frogs and toads, slugs, ugh! I had to pretend I liked them but ugh! boys will be boys. They had put them in this miniature garden to see where different animals went to different surroundings. I thought it was a very good idea!, well we had a laugh, only because they frightened me to death. After speaking to them first I felt inclined to stay with them just because I had got to know them straight away but I decided to go and try to talk to some others but well I found them to turn to ice at the thought of me talking to them, worrying whether they were the ones I was going to choose. Still I don't blame them, I remember when I was their age, sitting on one of those tiny chairs sprawled over my book so the teacher couldn't see my writing, then all of a sudden I would sense a teacher or somebody looking over my shoulder, I would feel a hot flush go to my cheeks as I blush to myself, meanwhile my heart's going ten to the dozen.

I decided to look around and see some of the work the children had done, yet again I got fed up of that. Some of the girls were drawing pictures and then colouring them in with wax crayons. I was dying to do some drawing or painting or, well to admit it, I was dying to try what they were doing, so I went and got a piece of paper and sat in the corner where I thought nobody could see me. I was happily drawing away when I heard giggling. I looked up and saw a crowd of girls watching me draw. One of the girls said 'what's that Carol' and I asked them to guess what I was drawing, not knowing that when I had finished they were still guessing. I had drawn a rose with lots of leaves around it, but the children thought it was a lettuce with privet leaves around it. We had lots of laughs and a few not so funny jokes about my drawing. This is where the relationship between the children and I began. They started calling me Carol and laughing and joking, I knew I had started something.

They all went to break and I stayed and coloured my drawing. I had nearly finished my lovely bright red rose with bright green leaves and a blue background when the children came back in. Well, was I shocked at the comments I got from 10–11-year-old kids.
(a) Oh Carol that's absolutely fabulous,
(b) Oh isn't that beautiful Carol,
(c) Oh Carol! so on and so on. I felt rather an artist.
One girl gave me a good talking to and told me (told me) mind you that I should be an art teacher and go and teach them.

After finishing the drawing somebody wanted the pleasure of screwing my so-called fabulous picture up. This was to make cracks in the wax to give an old looking effect.

The kids argued over screwing it up, until of course Byron spoke up 'let me have the pleasure please' so he stood there in front of me screwing it up while the kids watched my face drop. After he ironed it and I painted it, I was told it looked very nice. After that I got on great with the kids. I was quite amazed with the difference it had made just joining in with them. It was dinner and they said goodbye. Mike came to pick us up.

I don't think I've ever read a more truthful account of the transition from stranger to friend, or observer to participant, whether in the context of a primary school classroom or elsewhere. It opens with the desperation that accompanies a sense that the people you want to get to know are at heart inaccessible. It picks out the constricting shame and embarrassment small children often feel at an invasion of the privacy of their work, especially of their writing – a vital insight to anyone who wants to teach.

It acknowledges, wryly, the difficulty of sharing those pleasures of others which touch upon your own squeamishness. And then, out of an awareness of the stubborn self-absorption of this classroom of children emerges a beautifully precise and unforced appreciation of how a relationship can begin.

Carols' technique was to assume the same self-absorption as the others, drawing away alone in a corner – an intuition I had in no way hinted at to her and would probably have imagined to be fruitless. The effects it had on the children are noted with great faithfulness and clarity – from giggling to joking to calling her by name and finally to congratulation and serious conversation. When she 'joined in' Carol had not yet read what I had written in her book about 'taking your own drawings along with you and doing them alongside the children', but even if she had, I would not have foreseen just how she would set about joining in nor how clearly she would perceive the significance of her action.

Besides its central perception, Carol's piece is full of incidental appreciation of children's responses. She shows an immediate understanding of the importance of playfulness – of interpreting the rose as a lettuce, of 'the pleasure of screwing my so-called fabulous picture up'. She is aware, too, of the element of competitiveness and desire for recognition in the repetitive fulsomeness of the children's responses to her work and even, on a later occasion, to her clothes.

'Then after all these remarks a strange thing happened. A girl said that's a beautiful bracelet Carol, I do like it very much, and I said thank you. Then another girl proceeded in saying I do like your necklace Carol it's very pretty, I said thank you. THEN Oh Carol I like your shirt, then, I like your trousers, I like your shoes and so on. It was very funny, it was like after one said it the others felt they had to say something to get a thank you from me or something like that.'

Later still, chatting over another day's visit, Carol told me of the girl who'd sat next to her most of the morning, constantly looking over her work and saying how lovely it was and how much inferior her own work was by comparison. Once, when Carol had failed to reassure her the girl, after a pause, had added half to herself 'perhaps mine isn't really so bad'. We spent quite a time on the significance of the reaction.

Six weeks have passed since our first visit to Dunton Bassett and I can begin to reflect on what each of us has achieved so far out of our experience. Part of Carol's achievement, I think, is to have rediscovered her own childhood. It may even be just because she had rediscovered her own childhood that she has also discovered how to enter imaginatively into the childhood of others and so how to talk to children and work with them and study them. Each discovery has emerged in part out of experience and intuition and in part out of reflecting on experience and intuition in talk and in writing. And both the talk and the writing have been 'conversational' in essence and in tone.

As for me, I feel that, reading what Carol has written, talking over her experience with her and spending some time in the same classroom myself, has enriched my understanding of how to observe children and how to create relationships with them, in ways which I would not have discovered for myself.

When it comes to our future course of study I can only make the most preliminary observations. In a sense I know perfectly well what kind of direction I would like it to take. I would like to help Carol to deepen her understanding of the class by developing further those techniques of observation and participation whose essence she had already understood intuitively. I would like to help her to develop the skills of teaching. I also hope that eventually she will begin to investigate at a more general level the nature of cognitive growth. I am equally certain that all of these lines of development will prove to be lines of development for me as well as for Carol.

One important step is to try to involve the teacher of the class she is working in more directly with her own study. By his example and his conversation he would be able to help her more than anyone I know towards a general understanding of how small children learn. Another step, of course, is to interest her in the literature of child development. I have started by asking her to look over a beautiful short study of kindergarten children by Frances Hawkins, *The Logic of Action*, which I will later work through with her.

However, the literature presents innumerable problems, both in general because of its insupportable abstractions and its impoverished vocabulary, and in particular because Carol is one of those people whose extreme slowness at reading has developed into a genuine aversion to it. Nonetheless I don't despair of being able in some measure to resolve the reading problem. But what I know I must try to avoid at all costs is the splitting apart of the generalisations and the conceptualisations from that intuitive grasp of particularity which has been Carol's supreme advantage over the past few weeks.

It is enormously difficult for secondary school teachers like myself to avoid this splitting of knowledge. The shift into a formal mode of learning is so often accompanied by a dry didacticism in which contact with particular forms of life is lost. Techniques abound, concepts proliferate, but somehow they never lead back to observation and participation in those particular circumstances where it is necessary once more to search and explore, with an open mind, wide sympathy and as much imagination as one can muster.

This stage of transition to more formal modes of learning marks the point at which so many of my own students' fruitful experiences seem to wither away. Often our more sympathetic critics tell us that this is because we have ignored the need for precision in learning after the initial romance, or because we have underestimated the necessary grind inherent in any effort at intellectual mastery. Part of my answer would be to point once more to Carol's writing and talking. Informality does not imply carelessness nor any lack of intellectual control. I would point to the lack of irrelevancies in the extract I have quoted from her diary, and to its sharp sense of what is significant. It is a piece of critical discrimination of a high order. Another part of my answer would be to suggest the interconnectedness of imaginative insight and patient toil. It is not a matter of one succeeding the other but of both being part of each other.

However, I would be prepared to concede that the criticism has a certain force. Yet it should not disguise the more fundamental problem. For the re-integration of formal and informal modes of learning, of the lecture and the conversation if you like, itself requires a substantial reconstruction of knowledge. Somehow or other we are seeking to extend a power of generalisation and conceptualisation without losing the strength of an understanding which is rooted in a sense of particularity. But how?

Just once or twice over the past four years of teaching at Countesthorpe I feel that I have perhaps succeeded in this task. For example, I think of a student who studied some of the problems of old people, the mentally handicapped and 'disadvantaged' children, starting from a particular sequence of personal experiences, extending them to embrace the theoretical perspectives of a sociologist such as Peter Townsend as illustrated in his essays on 'The Social Minority', and returning again to the personal world and its obsessions and fascinations. Such successes owe more to luck than judgement. I am not yet in a position to analyse them or generalise from them as I would wish. I hope that Carol's work will be one of the successes when it is completed. At present all I can say is that it has started well. I have tried to work out why in this article. Now, I hope that others may be able to describe more ambitious and more complete examples of a similar pattern of learning. We need many descriptions and many analyses. Then perhaps we will begin to see more clearly what we need to do.

PART III
STUDENTS' REFLECTIONS

9

How I Found My Education

BARBARA SMITH

*BARBARA SMITH is a sixth form student. She arrived at Countes-
thorpe while still of high school age and was 14 when the first 'teams'
were formed. She therefore experienced the transition from comparative instability in the opening two years to the strong bonds evolved in
that development. Her article was written after the later transitional
period of moving out of her 'team' into the relatively unsupported
climate of the sixth.*

I would now regard my fourth year as the beginning of my education. We
were presented with the innovation of teams. The fourth year was split
in two, forming two teams – 4M and 4B, each with their individual
characteristics, which developed over the two years. This new pattern of
working took some time to get used to, although a feeling of security prevailed throughout. Also, at this stage the fourth-year intake from South
Wigston High School joined us, so we had different people to get used to
as well as the teams.

Each student spent basically ten lessons a week working in the team,
on work revolving mainly around English, social studies and maths.
Options for specialist subjects were offered in the other ten lessons. Timetables varied to suit the individual person. Some people spent more than
ten lessons a week in the team area, others may have spent more time
outside the team.

As I can remember it, we all started off on the same piece of work. We
had to write our autobiographies and also compile our family trees, if
that was possible. This gave the tutors an opportunity for getting to
know their students and their individual backgrounds, and acted as a
starting point for work which was to follow.

After completing my autobiography, I couldn't really think of any
work I could continue with. We started working through worksheets in
social studies based upon the family, to coincide with the work we had
done ourselves on our own families. My tutor suggested that as I was
particularly interested in music at the time, I might consider working on
a project involving some kind of musical aspects. I took up this idea, feel-

ing quite enthusiastic at the time, although only because I couldn't think of anything else to do.

In February 1973 the beginning of a phase of emotional disruption, disillusion, but all the same a lingering feeling of hope filled the air at Countesthorpe. A report had appeared on the front page of the local paper, condemning the College and all that it stood for, attacking the staff and the principal, as well as the students. This initial article filled me with bitter anger. The words in front of me just wouldn't sink in because I knew they were not true. I wanted to turn my eyes away, to look again and find that they didn't exist. A friend and I wrote a letter to the same paper. It was published, followed by many others from students and parents complaining of the undue criticisms made towards us.

For months after this we suffered these sickening attacks. I was lucky in having parents who thoroughly supported the school, but what about others who were really attached to the school and went home the next minute only to hear their parents calling the school every name under the sun?

However, although I would like to emphasise the importance that this particular period of time eventually played upon my education in the team, I do not think it is necessary for me to concentrate upon the subject to any deeper extent. The team was proving to be the basis of a continuous dialogue between myself, my tutor, and the outside world. I became interested in researching into the history of Blaby, the village where I had lived for a number of years. I decided to base my project upon Blaby in the 1700s, and became deeply involved in this work through reading various books, looking over many old documents through visits to the Leicester archives and looking at the church registers of that period of time. Through this work I was re-creating a picture of the past myself, with my tutor's advice. I think it would be true to say that the experience and interest of probing into the past in this way, was just as valuable to my tutor as it was to myself.

At the same time my interest in education had grown. By the time I entered the fifth year it had grown to such a considerable extent that it overtook my interest in the history of Blaby. I started to go to standing committee meetings and wanted to work around this interest in education. I experienced an incredible feeling of wanting to find out for myself, finding out through other people, along with the guidance that my tutor offered me. His guidance came over through a confidence in us both to converse freely, without the teacher ever playing the dominant role. If I lost my sense of direction and wasn't sure where to go next he would go through the alternatives with me. Through a zest in us both, and indeed from the tutor to the rest of the group, we found the key to learning and the answer to a personal knowledge. Learning became a dynamic experience through the spontaneity, observation and participatory values present in the team, and above all, through the conversation or continuous dialogue between teacher and student.

I read *Summerhill* by A. S. Neill, and after this my thoughts on education became even deeper. My ideas changed completely or maybe it was just that I had never thought of ideas such as Neill put together in his books. I wanted to strengthen my bond towards Countesthorpe and develop my own ideas towards life in general. I started a project based upon the Leicestershire plan but I lost interest in this idea, mainly due to general lack of information, or perhaps it was a lack of the particular kind of information I wanted. I wanted to get beyond the outline of the plan to the deeper questions of education in Leicestershire but I found that people were not as co-operative as I hoped. I went to interview a man at County Hall but he wouldn't tell me very much. He kept asking me questions instead of letting me ask him. I then decided to widen the scope of this project to 'A. S. Neill and Progressive Education'. I studied his background, the development of Neill's ideas and the development of Summerhill and its influence on other progressive schools. I enjoyed this work more than any I had previously done, and it has been the main influence on my ideas and interests since I started it, plus the fact that it has proved to be a very necessary part of my understanding, awareness and knowledge.

The team was a place where you could return to, where there was usually someone around to talk to. It was the root from which our personalities or characters developed. It was the generator for reconstructing our past, fitting it into the present and preparing us for the future. Maybe I became too attached to the team. I can think of a number of occasions when I just wanted to carry on working in the team area rather than go to specialist lessons although I had opted for them. My work may have suffered in some of those subjects studied outside the team but I wouldn't say that I regret concentrating on the subjects I studied in the team rather than on the others because it would have had a damaging effect on my learning patterns to have studied the things I was not interested in.

The end of 5M was very sad. Entry into the sixth form has been more disillusioning than any other part of my education. For the first few months I missed the team to such an incredible extent that I actually pondered upon the thought of leaving. There was no sense of spontaneity, no zest for learning, nothing to catch you if you felt fed up and wanted to fall back into something firm rather than boredom.

When we left the team it seemed that our only remaining contacts from the last two years were our old tutors. I still see my old tutor apart from the fact that he teaches me sociology. We carry on our dialogue.

Indeed, the team promoted my innermost strengths, discovered and developed my particular interests and helped me on the way to rational thinking (sometimes not so rational). It helped me to clarify my thoughts and my ideas through putting them into words. It offered me the courage to persist in overcoming my weaknesses. It gave me the urge to find out or myself. We were never forced into specified moulds, but we were presented with a situation and it was up to us, along with our tutors to make the most of it. There were always new links, new passages, new directions, new insights, differing reasons, varying patterns available to us.

Compulsion seems like a kind of madness, an insanity when I think of Countesthorpe and its room for flexibility and freedom.

Countesthorpe is the school. The teams are the schools within the school and that was where I found my education.

10

Looking Back from University

JOSIE HATSWELL

JOSIE HATSWELL experienced the first four years of Countesthorpe, entering at 14, and being too late to benefit from working within a 'team'. In the sixth form she was able to combine studies for A levels with such diverse activities as playing Olivia in Twelfth Night, *and representing her fellow students as guest at the First International Convention on Options in Public Education at Minneapolis in 1973. After one year at university she wrote commenting on her four years at Countesthorpe and her reactions to undergraduate life.*

I have enjoyed the past year so much at college and I wouldn't have missed it for anything and similarly, I feel the same way about the time I spent at Countesthorpe.

This year, as I have talked with people from other backgrounds, I think I have maintained an almost conceited opinion of the education I have experienced. Many people, when I've spoken about Countesthorpe, have more or less accused me of lying and refuse to believe that such a school exists, but then most people have come round in the end and have become very interested in it.

A lot of people at City come from public schools and they, in particular, have got a very different attitude to work to mine. They are far more conscientious than me and I think they will achieve better marks in the exams than me. Actually, I think examinations is one of the things that Countesthorpe has let me down on. Although I strongly believe that examinations are futile and an unrealistic way of assessing ability, the fact remains that many institutions, including the City University, are still structured around an examination system. And for me, who has not had all the traditional build-up year after year for O and A levels, I find it rather disconcerting to have to sit very traditional examinations in a big, ugly hall and am definitely at a disadvantage.

Something that I do miss terribly about Countesthorpe is the relationship between staff and students and everything that it entails. It took me a long time to get used to having a lecturer who stood in front of me for an hour and then walked out again, remaining an anonymous talking machine throughout. I really have no personal contact with any of the academic staff except my tutor – and that is minimal and formal.

The students' union does fulfil some of the functions of the student/staff relationship at Countesthorpe in that it provides welfare services, people who are always ready to listen to any problems and of course lots of social activities; but at the same time as giving the students unity it is emphasising the polarisation between the academic staff and students, which is not congruent with Countesthorpe ideals. And worse still, it doesn't seem to have occurred to anyone that it should be any different.

I still feel a highly privileged individual to have been a student at Countesthorpe College and I am sure that without it, I would be a far less enterprising person than I am now. If nothing else, I think it has given me the ability to question the right of lecturers to tell me that I am wrong and that they are right, when many of them seem more concerned about my bad spelling and grammar than the actual content of essays.

Next year I am doing a course that deals specifically with the sociology of education, which I'm sure I will find very enjoyable!

Well, I hope these brief comments are of some use to you, I certainly hope that Countesthorpe continues to give people the opportunities that it has given me.

11

Seen and Not Heard

A comment on learning through discussion

HAZEL OXLEY

HAZEL OXLEY left school at 15. Being a secondary modern pupil, she knew from the age of 10 that she was an 11–plus failure, and although among the majority of children to share that condition, she was aware of deemed deficiency for twenty years. At that point she joined the growing number of adults taking places in day school along-side the full-time day students at Countesthorpe, while her own two children were at school. With ambitions to become a teacher herself, she embarked upon O and A level courses, completing them in one year with excellent results. What it feels like to break through the sense of failure and inferiority imposed by the school system on a child is conveyed in an article she wrote between sitting for those exams.

During my fifteen years' absence from school I hadn't thought much about teaching methods and the evolutions talking place within our schools. Although I have children of my own at school, and I gradually became aware that methods had changed, for some indistinct reason I didn't connect the change with secondary education. In spite of reading various newspaper reports from time to time, the reality of it all was to me obscure. Therefore when I did return to school my first impressions were mixed and ranged from astonishment and some strangeness to eventual joy and respect. For instance, to be confronted by members of staff who dressed informally and were addressed by their first names went against the grain of all my preconceptions. In my experience teachers were remote figures dressed in three-piece suits or respectable dresses and always wearing 'sensible shoes'. They existed (amongst other things) to set an example to the pupils and always demanded Sir or Miss; of course we knew their first names but never dared breathe them within their earshot.

I went to a secondary modern school which until the year I moved up from the junior department had been a county senior school. The transition to secondary modern was accomplished by the acquisition of a climbing frame, some climbing ropes and an agility mat. We too were not subjected to wearing a uniform. That is to say a uniform was not compulsory, but one existed. It took the form of blouses and skirts made in the needlework classes from antique patterns. The colour of the resulting monstrosities depended upon the house to which one belonged, as my house colour was yellow – I never wore a uniform. However, had I passed my 11-plus I would no doubt have bravely and proudly sported the prerogative of the grammar schools, a uniform, many of them no less monstrous in appearance. No doubt too I would have been a different person, for to fail the 11-plus was to fail totally. Most of the professional jobs became impossible to contemplate, but a more disastrous effect only became apparent in later life, the inability to think on one's feet, a talent which is absolutely essential if one is to survive the 'Human Jungle' and be considered a success. In short we were sold out and destined to become also-rans, little cogs, never amongst the winners.

Condemned to the secondary modern I suppose in many ways I escaped much of the formal type of teaching which was common in the grammar school system. The opportunities to take O level and A level examinations being non-existent, we were not crammed with facts for examination purposes, but nevertheless we had 'teacher' at the blackboard and 'class' regimented in rows in the 'classroom'. Subjects were hurled at us and discussion frowned upon, one either sank or swam; in the school we had streaming, A, B, C and D and to my eternal astonishment the powers-that-be deemed I should be allowed to perform the impossible, the unheard of, and move from a B stream into an A stream at the beginning of my third year, a feat only to be compared with transferring from a secondary modern to a grammar school at 15 years old. Consequently my last two years at school were spent desperately trying to catch up to A class standard hampered by the desire not to appear too stupid and being unable to ask a sufficient number of questions. In order to ask questions one had to 'run the gauntlet' as it were and choose between two evils, the ridicule of an entire class for the poor unfortunate or the teacher's barely concealed impatience that one should fail to understand a carefully explained problem; in either eventuality to ask anything at all equalled ignorance, not a healthy and questioning mind.

To enter Countesthorpe College with my background was a challenge to both sides. Convinced of my inability as an 11-plus failure to possess O levels and A levels, I timorously embarked upon the language and literature courses, backed and pushed by encouragement from family and friends. My preconceptions seem hilarious now after several months of exposure to the school, but I was slightly afraid, deferential and aggressive by turns as new situations developed.

The open plan of the school fits the teaching methods and provides a marked contrast to the ways in which I was taught. The openness of the areas, the lack of rows of desks in the rooms and the teaching methods employed, offered for me a whole new world, one I never thought existed. To be taught, or rather to learn in such surroundings is so much more pleasurable. By degrees I became accustomed to all these novel features, although for quite a while I fully expected the mirage to dissolve and once again be confronted by desk, blackboard and teacher.

Learning through discussion brought a whole new aspect to bear upon the subjects which I studied and I feel one from which I certainly would have benefited in my own school days had there been the opportunity for me to receive this type of education. I have thoroughly enjoyed the experience and for the first time in my life I have had to develop the discipline of self-discipline in relation to academic work.

It seems ironic that the mechanics of this self-discipline should be made so obvious at Countesthorpe and yet so shrouded in mystery for me before. Having been encouraged in the art of self-discipline it leaves me not so much in a completed state of mind at the end of my courses as at the beginning of an ever-branching road, one which I should like to see become open to all.

PART IV
THE COMMUNITY

Community education has many forms and it is unlikely that any one centre or college will ever reflect quite the same interpretation of this concept as any other. It is partly to do with lifelong education, partly to do with people becoming involved in the provision for their own needs.

All part-time users of Countesthorpe College. about a thousand in number, have representation on its community council. The council elects its own officers and three members who sit on the governing body. Each year at the council's AGM some prepared attempt is made to present members with illustrations of the College's activities. In the Autumn of 1974 Christine English gave a short talk which was the basis for the next article.

CHRISTINE ENGLISH, who 'only came for the creche', recounted how she, then her children and her husband, became involved in a whole range of activities. Some of these entailed conceptual exploration, some developed new skills, some enabled the use of existing but under-used abilities in order to provide for other members of the community. Perhaps most significantly – Christine was drawn into the discussion and planning that must be an essential element in any true community education, self-determining and self-helping.

Christine English is not entirely typical in the degree of her involvement, but she sums up in her own personal recollection what is collectively typical. Her own exclamation 'Now I think I can do anything' may not be the exaggeration she intended it to be. The community college can enable people to discover new competence and new confidence by taking things on in co-operation with each other, and finding they can do them.

12

'I Only Came for the Creche'

CHRISTINE ENGLISH

I really only came to Countesthorpe College for the creche. We had recently moved to Countesthorpe and I had a son who, after spending his first twenty months of life cooped up in a flat, was in need of socialising, as was his rather desperate mother.

My involvement with Countesthorpe College started with enrolment night in August/September 1972. Whilst innocently enrolling for a silversmithing course I noticed a little handwritten notice above one of the tables – 'Creche helpers needed. See Ann Tester.' I hadn't actually thought of doing this sort of thing but suddenly it seemed an ideal way of getting Max to mix with other children and for myself, now beginning to feel rather stagnant from a lack of interest outside my family, a way of getting out of my home and involved with other people. I never imagined quite how involved I was to become.

For the first fourteen months I attended my night school class and helped out with the Thursday morning creche and that was about it. Then, I think in late January, a friend who knew I'd done a lot of catering work before my marriage, said 'Christine, can you help me out? Just this once?' That was it. Apparently the first family day had been arranged and she and her husband, both caterers, were to have looked after feeding the expected masses.

I said I'd help and that was my entry into ensuing family days and holiday activities. The family day was a new concept in the work of the community college. The idea was not just to get the children there for a full Sunday, but also their parents. It was hoped that some of us would take part with our children and some help with activities. The response was good. When the doors opened for enrolment at 10.30 we were greeted with a long queue of people waiting to try out this latest venture. We were thrilled. A lot of planning had gone into the day and we would all have been bitterly disappointed if no one had arrived.

Activities were similar to previous holiday activities but scaled down. We had a creche for the under-7s, puppet-making, art, ornamental gardens in saucers, 'pirates', football, chess, pottery, drama for big and little ones and numerous other activities. To enrol for one activity, we charged one new penny. We also cooked midday meals at a very nominal price. We had a choice of soup, sausages, hamburgers, beans, baked potatoes, sandwiches, ice-cream and drinks. It disappeared in a flash. I'd never have believe such small tummies could put away such huge quantities of food. During the lunch period, the recreation room was also open and table tennis and other games were played. The tuck-shop was also there for snacks.

At the end of the day everyone met in the crescent area and had a well-earned cup of coffee and a quiet chat. I think we all felt the day had been successful, if totally exhausting.

We followed this venture up with other family days, all equally success-ful. For the last one that I was able to take part in we decided to have a theme. As the day we chose happened to fall on the Chinese New Year we said we'd use that. I think probably more work went into preparing this day than any other. We decided we had to be authentic, so all our informa-tion had to be correct. A group of us spent an evening at the Education Resources Centre learning all we could about the Chinese. None of us realised just how much there was to know about their culture. However, the day arrived, and we put on Chinese puppet-making, masks, Chinese cookery, pottery, Chinese games, such as mah-jong and chess. We had an exhibition of Chinese articles and a beautiful display and demonstra-tion of Chinese musical instruments. We had a very good film on China, and some people even learnt to write some Chinese. We had a Chinese lunch, which was great fun: I'd never imagined I would cook Chinese food for 150 people. Now I think I can do anything.

I think I ought to add here that the creche that started off in two small rooms to cater for 0–7-year-olds, had by this time become something of note. It now took over three rooms and most of the main crescent area, a very large area of the College. These little ones were able to do their own thing all day. They had water-play, clay, painting, and a small toy area and a large careering-round area. They loved it. My children (by this time I had two) used to spend the whole day there and never wanted to leave – a compliment to those in charge, if ever there was one. The day finished with the drama people and the creche, who had made two lovely dragons going around the College, collecting up bodies and taking them down to the drama workshop where they performed the play they had been practis-ing all day. It was really fun.

I also became involved in successive Easter and summer holiday activi-ties. These were run at Easter for three days and during the summer vacation for three days in three consecutive weeks. We did pretty well the same things as for the family days except that of course activities could run into the next day, so projects could be undertaken. During one summer vacation the pottery people decided to build their own kiln outside and do all their firing there. It was very successful. We also had trips to local places of interest. The activities were really too numerous to mention in detail. I would like to add that all these activities are run by volunteers, mothers like myself, and members of staff who felt they could stand the extra time in school.

The holiday activities were probably the most taxing as they were so concentrated – three days a week for three weeks is quite hard work. Any work I needed to do at home was ignored and my husband even came up to the College for his lunch, much to everyone's amusement. I'm afraid that once home, I collapsed, as did Max and Hannah. We all found though, that at the end of the three weeks, we missed it. The children found it hard to settle down with me again and I found it equally hard to settle down to my routine of work at home.

Hannah, my second child, was most accommodating, and was born during half-term. Thus, she joined the creche straight from birth, and in fact spent the greater part of her first two years of life in the College. Even Max's nursery schooling was fitted in around the regular creche that I still helped with. I think he enjoyed it equally as much as his nursery school.

There were several activities at the College aimed at helping the young mother stuck at home. We had what was called 'Morning Break', a two-hour morning session for the creche where we had guest speakers on various subjects, from local theatre to toddlers' tantrums. There was always a discussion period and the morning proved very valuable to many mothers. We also had one afternoon a week when mothers and children swarmed into the recreation area of the College. The children played in the large creche area, supervised by helpers and mothers, while other mothers simply chatted and had a coffee. This was always well-supported as there was obviously a need in the village for something of this sort. We had the odd coffee morning too with a bring-and-buy sale to raise money to buy toys for the creche, always an expense and always needed.

There was always something going on. On reflection, I think I probably spent as much if not more time at the College than at home. My husband tells me I frequently did.

Perhaps I should add at this point that both my husband and I were attending some interesting night school courses. We did two very good sociology courses, something I'd always wanted to do. Later we learnt a great deal about the methods of teaching in secondary education through a series of lectures by tutors from both outside and within the College. [*This was one of the courses arranged in collaboration with the University of Leicester extra-mural department. Ed.*] It was fascinating, and certainly gave us an insight into education today.

I also became involved with the executive committee of the College, and even to my horror one evening gave a talk, on similar lines to those of this article, to the community council. [*The representative body of community users of the college. Ed.*] Had anyone told me that I would become quite so involved in two years, I never would have believed it.

I have to say that my time spent at Countesthorpe College was a happy and fulfilling one, and really went to prove that education within the community is a lifelong one. Unhappily I no longer live in Countesthorpe. My husband's job has taken us to Jamaica, so here I look for another involvement and I wonder if I shall find anything quite the same.

13

A Parent Reflects

GEOFFREY TAYLOR

GEOFFREY TAYLOR, is a general practitioner. Educated at the Wyggeston School, Leicester, he read Medicine at Cambridge and served in the Royal Navy. He lives in Countesthorpe. He has three children, the eldest of whom studied at Countesthorpe College 1970–5 and then entered Trinity Hall Cambridge to read medicine. His second son is in the sixth form of the college. Dr Taylor has been chairman of the governing body since it was first convened.

Like many other parents, our first acquaintance with Countesthorpe College was in the summer of 1970. This was at a meeting held in one of the neighbouring junior schools to introduce the warden and his senior staff of the school which our two elder children would attend in the autumn. There was at this time a considerable amount of publicity in both local and national press which appeared to emphasise the innovations and new approaches to education which were to be implemented. The reaction to this could either be enthusiasm for a brave new approach or apprehension at the loss of a well-known, well-remembered and well-tried system.

The concept of participation and commitment in decision-making by the whole school community, of a modern curriculum with a basic core and additional options with increasing pupil responsibility for their own destiny in a comprehensive, coeducational, community school, seemed to me an ideal of education worthy of support in preparing all our young people for the world of today and tomorrow.

By the time the governors first met in January 1971 there was good cause for disquiet; the buildings and fitments already showed evidence of misuse. There was little evidence of that order and stability in the school community necessary to allow the ideals to be put into practice. The standard of behaviour both in and out of school left much to be desired and at times we might be excused for feeling that the staff were so concerned not to enforce trivial and ridiculous school rules that they were not prepared to support any standards at all. While the sincerity, ability and enthusiasm of the staff could not be doubted they appeared to lack tact and experience and the ability to convince parents in simple terms what their aims and objectives were.

What was at fault? Was it the principles, their implementation or both? The initial response of governors was equally divided and events of that first year did nothing to increase confidence.

By the time John Watts was appointed principle in the spring of 1972 there were a number of serious problems to be overcome. Morale was low and the ripples of discontent from parents and community were getting stronger.

Accepting the principles, the task of making them work was going to be long and difficult. The solution to some problems was achieved early with the establishment and implementation of the necessary organisation.

Other problems required time. Time to think through the ideas, to gain confidence, to persuade and influence attitudes and to build the necessary organisation. And of time there was not enough.

The storm of discontent broke in the spring of 1973. Was it disappointment that progress was too slow, or that the new principles had not been discarded and the school returned to a more reputable tradition?

Angry and emotional meetings took place of those for and against the school, avidly reported in the local press which had amassed a huge file of evidence. The waves of discontent spread to involve politicians at local and national level and culminated in the demand for an inquiry and the full inspection of the school which took place at the end of 1973.

But the tide had turned. A well-attended parents meeting in June 1974 at which the director of education presented a very full and frank appraisal of the problems facing the school finished with a strong expression of confidence in the principal and his staff. The school was now the upper school for 14- to 18-year-olds for which it had originally been intended. Staff and pupils realised that school property must be respected; what was restored must be conserved. Acceptable and sensible standards of behaviour were being enforced and anti-social behaviour strongly discouraged. Examination results were beginning to show an encouraging response to the attitudes to work and academic achievement.

Not that I would wish to suggest that all problems are solved and all battles won, we are still far from any such complacent state – rather that a fair course has now been set. For if Countesthorpe is to remain true to its principles it must always be ready critically to examine what its objectives and achievements have been and be prepared to implement change to gain improvement, and perhaps remain a little controversial in the process.

The anger of two years ago has given place to an increased understanding and toleration between teachers and parents but still with reservations and some opposition. The governors who in the last five years have spent many long and anxious hours in debate have expressed their confidence in the College and its principal.

We have passed through five turbulent years : times of difficulty, doubt and sometimes near-despair. Perhaps it would be wise to reflect how far the success of any system of education depends on the enthusiasm and integrity of those involved, while so much of the social and academic achievement of the pupils depends on the example, attitude and encouragement of the parents. I trust that we are now embarked on a future of amicable and constructive co-operation between staff, parents and governors to ensure that we achieve the best for all our children.

PART V
TEACHING IN A DEMOCRATIC SCHOOL

THE DEMOCRATIC GOVERNMENT

There are certain statutory requirements of any school. For instance, every school must keep registers, a log book and a punishment book (even if, as here, the teachers administer no corporal punishment). Attendance is compulsory up to 16. The local education authority also decides the nature, age-range and design of a school. The head of a school is given control of the internal organisation, management and discipline. The governing body has general direction of the conduct and curriculum, with the requirement that there shall be full consultation at all times between the head and the chairman of governors.

How the head arranges the internal organisation is left to him, so long as he accepts his contracted accountability and all goes well. At Countesthorpe, the principal has sought to make the running of the College and the decision of policy as fully participatory as possible.

What lies behind the thinking and how this operates in pratice is covered in the following three articles.

14

A Teacher's Work at Countesthorpe

DAVE CLAIDEN

*DAVE CLAIDEN read English and philosophy at the University of
Sussex. He was appointed when Countesthorpe opened, to teach
English and drama. He was chosen by the teaching staff as one of their
two nominees on the governing body when that first became possible in
1975 under revised articles.*

*His article describes the complexity of involvement in the College's
life and work that is typical of what elsewhere might have been an
'assistant' teacher's role.*

I work in the 5/1 team: 108 fifth-year students of comprehensive ability
and five teachers. Our timetable is divided into twenty periods, ten of
which are taken for 'team time' that covers English, social studies and
mathematics, as well as other activities (some difficult to classify) which
are considered valuable by teachers, students or both. Drama, outdoor
pursuits (done jointly with a specialist teacher), activities with technolo-
gical, scientific or artistic components – the camera obscura, pin-hole
cameras, painting and construction, hot-air balloons, photograms, tape-
recording, microscope work and field studies, are some examples that come
readily to mind.

The team is staffed by a mathematician, two social studies teachers, an
English teacher and a fifth with a degree in psychology; we are not
specialists in all the areas in which we work.

So as teachers we are often, literally, learning. The school has its
teachers, scientists, music specialist, linguists and craft teachers to whom
the students go for help in working when not in team time. (Although the
division between team time and specialist time is not hard and fast,
students can use team time to further work initiated in a specialist area.)

These teachers also provide team teachers with valuable resources –
materials or expertise – for work in the teams. A current example may
make the process clear.

I have a small group of students who wished to make a film shot against
a static design. We needed to know the cheapest way of producing the
design that could be removed with the minimum fuss, as the group decided

that not everyone might wish to live with the design as a permanent feature of their environment. I did not have the necessary knowledge, and the group had neither the time nor the money for lengthy experiments. It was an art teacher who provided the ideas about the methods and materials we are using.

As teachers we also learn from the other teachers in our team (for instance, I have recently helped out with some work on slide-rules for which I needed a refresher course from the maths teacher in our team) and it is also true to say, without being sentimental, that we learn from our students. Quite often I work with a student on a theme (perhaps in his or her social studies work – not something outside the mainstream of work) of which I have no prior superior knowledge. Indeed, the student sometimes has more knowledge than I have of the subject. It may be that I have more experience than a student of learning how to learn, and I see it as my job to aid the student with his methods of study, but students do produce perceptions from which I learn.

For instance, a boy undertook a study of Blaby, a local village, which taught me much about the local community : the pattern of work in Blaby, people's use of leisure time, an estimation of the adequacy of social service provision in Blaby and an assessment of the provision of facilities for different age-groups. The conclusions he came to altered my notion of how good a place Blaby is to live in.

A similar transference occurs sometimes with a filming or drama group. It is a student who points out why the improvisation is not satisfactory or why it has worked well. I am not saying that I have abdicated all responsibility for students' learning, that all learning is undertaken by the unaided student, but I do think that my role as a teacher is no longer that of a superior specialist, handing knowledge 'down', but rather that of engaging a student or group of students in a dialogue through which both the students' and teachers' understanding changes. Sometimes the 'dialogue' can be one-sided, sometimes it doesn't exist at all. Some students are reluctant to do anything and some insist on being told what to do, and in both cases I will often do just that, insist they do what I want them to do. But mutual learning is an aim and it is achieved in practice amid the failures to gain interest and to achieve worthwhile attainment.

The team is the main pastoral unit in the school as well as being the teaching base for the students. It is necessary to know the students well in order to work well with them in our way. The closeness of relationship between teachers and students in the team can, however, bring its problems. It calls, sometimes, for unusual objectivity in dealing with irritating students and the same quality is no doubt called for in students who have to face irritating teachers. However, by and large, our relationships are open, friendly, mostly honest and supportive. It is quite natural for students with problems to approach the staff in their team for sympathy and help (although we do have students, I suppose nearly all students at some time, who are hostile for a variety of reasons. However, even with hostile students, the relationship with staff is close, in that under the conditions of the team, staff learn much about the hostile student and his background.)

In this way, teachers do sometimes get drawn into the domestic lives of students. I can think of a case of a girl who has looked ill and unhappy all term and who, before seeing the school nurse, scratched her wrists. In an atmosphere of sympathy, the girl readily volunteered an account of the near break-up of her family during the summer holidays. Involvement of this kind can entail delicate decisions. Sometimes confidences are made that the student does not wish the parents to know about. The account a student gives of his or her home life does not always square with that of the parents. A teacher does not wish to be guilty of unwelcome interference – although in the case mentioned above the girl's mother made the first move and contacted the school to discuss her daughter's problems with us. In fact, in most cases of this kind, parents and teachers do cooperate. Sometimes a student will try to get a teacher to endorse a dislike of a parent, and sometimes a parent will encourage a student to dislike the school. It is easy to make mistakes.

It is easy to get 'over-involved' in the sense of dwelling too much on the problems and thereby, unintentionally, rubbing salt into the wound. We can forget that we meet students for only a short period in their lives and can easily begin an involvement that the student expects to last for longer than it can realistically be sustained.

However, in a school which encourages openness and friendliness in its relationships, students will treat teachers as sympathetic adults, and teachers will be carried into involvements of a personal rather than a scholastic nature. It seems to me right that this should be so; that the teacher who knows much about a student ought to be involved sympathetically alongside other professionals and not be merely a monitor, spotting problems when they arise. Indeed the atmosphere of openness and friendliness that enables the problems to be visible also ensures an active role for the teacher in their remedy.

Not all my work is done in the 5/I team nor with its students. In common with the other teachers in the team, I have teaching commitments outside it. I teach some sixth form, I work with the games department for one afternoon a week, and I work with some adults who come into the college to take courses alongside the students of school age. I am not conscious of any great difference between this group and the school-age students as far as teaching is concerned. Their presence in the classroom, however, makes me very much aware of a need to ensure that everything goes as well as it possibly can, for I do see these people as visitors from what has been, in part, a hostile community. Part of the job is to communicate to people outside the school our aims, and the fact that, in our view, these are being fulfilled.

This task is undertaken during visits to parents (a tutor tries to visit the parents of each student in his group at least once; this visit is not made solely to explain the school in a general way, but such questions do arise when discussing the specific concerns of parents for their child), through special meetings called for the purpose of explaining the workings of parts of the school, and through the activities and publications of the parent/teacher committee. This group has reprinted, for the benefit of parents, the recent *TES* articles about the school, and recently organised an open day for the purpose of raising money and displaying examples of work done in the school. These two activities perhaps mark a dichotomy within the committee, between fund-raising and explanation. Not all parents on the PTA committee would be convinced that part of its function is to explain the school's purposes, in principle or in practice. Some parents would say that the meetings we have called as a PTA to explain the workings of the school have not been very successful and have failed to attract particularly large audiences.

As far as the issue of parental involvement in the decision-making of the College is concerned, a general invitation is issued for them to attend and vote at the moots (the general meetings to decide the important matters of practice and principle governing the running of the College) but I think it true to say that there has been some reluctance among parents to take up the invitation and equally true that the staff have not advanced the matter particularly strongly.

However, both the activities of the PTA and the decision to allow parents to vote at moots mark an intention to involve parents in the running of the school in some way, to do more than just inform parents of how the school is run. But I feel that our thinking about this aspect of our role is in its infancy. In practice, at the moment, we do little more than listen seriously to individual parents and vote alongside parents at PTA meetings when choosing committees or allocating money raised by the association. Of course not everything at Countesthorpe is new.

I would shy away, too, from making grand claims for myself as a teacher working in the whole community. There are community activities at the College but, with the important exception of those adults who come in to take courses during the day, they are mainly a thing apart from the work being done by the 14–18-year-olds. The existence of the community activities does affect the teacher's role. He no longer has sovereign sway over facilities; he can't, for instance, arrange to use equipment or the drama areas without first consulting the adult groups who also use them. Some teachers do provide evening sessions in the College, but again, although there is an interest in examining the present distinctions between education for adolescents and education for adults, and also in looking at the separation of roles implied in the notion that teachers do the educating and other adults do the bringing up, I think it would be true to say that as teachers we haven't got very far in crystallising these notions and putting them into practice. However, the fact that we do consider these matters, collectively and individually, implies a way of seeing ourselves that is manifest in other areas of our activities. The 'assistant teacher' sees himself as having the right and the responsibility to evaluate what he is doing and to initiate and decide on principles and practices affecting the running of the school.

As far as the staff is concerned it is expected that everyone will participate in the decision-making processes of the school. There is internal disagreement over quite how 'true' is the democracy – whether or not everyone has equal access to information or whether some voices are more equal than others – but compared to a school where policy decisions are made by the head alone, or with an advisory body of senior staff, the teacher at Countesthorpe plays a far more active role in determining the circumstances of his work. For one term in four he has a place on the committee that meets weekly to determine matters concerning the everyday running of the school. He can vote in the moot, and all team and subject department matters are decided by collective decisions of the staff concerned. It is not that the teacher is given *carte blanche* to do whatever he likes, but that he has a right to a say in matters which need to be determined for all, ranging from dinner arrangements to proposals for mixed-age teams. The approach calls for an ability to accept personally unpleasant decisions on the one hand and requires a workable consensus-seeking approach on the other.

A collective approach runs through the teaching also. We have few classrooms into which we can disappear with a group and shut the door on the rest. Most of our teaching is done in large areas alongside other teachers. We have to get along with other teachers as well as students in the actual activity of teaching.

'Team-teaching' in our sense can range from an intuitive understanding with the teacher in the other half of the room – a common sense of purposes and timing – to projects for which teachers come together for the sole purpose of a particular activity. For example, I have just finished a play with two other teachers involving our three drama groups. It means teachers in the team deciding on a common approach to the use and care of the space and agreeing on common priorities for the term.

If a teacher is a tutor in a team he may well act as a mediator between his students and the staff in subject areas. He may have to resolve with the subject teacher difficulties that have arisen in the case of a particular student, or it may be that either the team or the subject area feel that arrangements between them are not working out. I can think of a recent case in which the sports department felt (quite rightly it now appears) that certain activities within our team were undercutting what they were trying to achieve. This difficulty was resolved by the sports staff and the team staff coming together, with no intervention from a hierarchy of heads of department or deputy heads. The head and deputy heads do step in to provide a mediation service if matters do break down, but it is not necessary that they do so, nor is a teacher obliged to hand the business to them. A teacher is bound by the general principles that he has had a say in constructing, carries part of the general responsibility for their execution, but also, in such a flexible institution, decides matters in particular areas with small groups of staff.

At its worst moments it all seems too much, there is so much to fulfil, there are too many meetings, and it doesn't work anyway. At its best, there is the excitement that comes from mutual learning that cannot result from any other form of teaching and a sense of accomplishment in having a say in an institution tackling such important matters.

15

Participatory Government — the Place of the Head

JOHN WATTS

JOHN WATTS *started teaching at Sawston Village College in Henry Morris's Cambridgeshire. He was head of English at Crown Woods Comprehensive School, London, and then in 1964, became first headmaster of Les Quennevais, a secondary and community school, in Jersey. He has also been involved in teacher-education as a lecturer at the University of London Institute of Education. Having watched Countesthorpe with interest and enthusiasm when it opened, he succeeded Tim McMullen as principal in 1972. Watts has published school-books, articles, and* Teaching, *an introduction to the life of a teacher (David & Charles, 1974). He has travelled as guest lecturer in Europe and Australasia.*

His article on 'The Role of the Head in a Participatory Democracy' is reprinted from The Role of the Head Teacher, *edited by Professor R. S. Peters (Routledge & Kegan Paul, 1976). In it, John Watts examines various structures of government in schools, old and new, and comments on the benefits and problems that arise, as he sees them, from the model adopted at Countesthorpe.*

Any head must delegate or disintergrate.

However, delegation may be executed in such a way that no real authority, only work-load, is passed out by the head. The crucial questions concern where the decisions are made and to whom decision-makers are accountable. Probably most heads today claim that their decisions are made in consultation, either with their deputies, some form of cabinet of faculty or .pastoral heads, or even with their whole staff. Yet none of this consultation constitutes participatory government in the sense in which I wish to speak of it, and which has been practised at Countesthorpe since it opened in 1970.

At that time of opening, the question was asked, 'How may we maintain an innovatory approach once we have embarked upon it?' It was not enough to have instituted a school with a number of radically new features; change was envisaged as a continuous process. Hierarchical organisations are relatively impervious to change. How were we to remain open to change? More particularly, whence would come the initiative and the inventiveness for change? If it were to come only from the top, how could it be adequate? However experienced a head and his senior staff might be, however reliable their judgement, what likelihood was there of their imaginations being fertile? Younger teachers are more likely to have ideas and propose innovations than their elders. The ideas may need the riddling of experience, expertise and judgement, but they must keep coming.

My experience with graduate teacher training left me worried about the number of young men and women, ones with initiative and a sense of service, who changed their minds about becoming teachers after the experience of school practice had revealed to them the extent to which the hierarchy in staff would stifle their ambition. 'Keep quiet and conform', was the message. They traded the securities of teaching for work with more risk, but a high demand for showing within a year or two what they could do with some opportunity for enterprise.

So the need to attract young teachers who want to get something done argues for their being given increased opportunity and responsibility. New developments in school place increased demands upon the teacher, and in particular he is required to forego much of the autonomy he formerly enjoyed in the classroom in order to plan and execute work jointly with groups of colleagues. What may have been acceptable in the closed classroom must be modified to balance the working of a team. With the general growth in the size of schools there is danger that the teacher may come to feel depersonalised and alienated. It is reasonable for him to expect, in return for meeting new demands, a new degree of control in determining the conditions under which he works (particularly concerning the distribution of available resources), whom he works with, and in what sort of atmosphere. Control of, and responsibility for, these conditions may be expected to produce increased satisfaction and dignity.

There are of course other arguments for reducing the powers normally invested in the head. Although a newly appointed head may be the most effective agent for rapid change in a school, his impetus will be lost within five years. The school may then have to wait for one or two decades to make another lurch forward.

Public demands for changes in the school may lead increasingly to ways being found to by-pass the head and introduce change-agents from outside. These may prove to be less gentle than the advisers and Schools Council project officers encountered up till now.

The school needs equally well to be protected from the destructive wake that may be left by the progressive reforming head who has failed to win a consensus of support from the staff, students and parents. An authoritarian progressive will usually come unstuck when outside agencies can exploit the division he has created among his staff. When this happens the reform aimed for by the head is thwarted, the power passes out of the school even to the point of its closing down and, more to the point, children suffer.

We are thus faced with the question of which way the head's powers will be redeployed. Will they spread to external authority, or will they be shared within school? In depicting what happens when shared internally at Countesthorpe, I wish first to outline the powers in question, then to consider the reshaped role of the head, then to look at the problems I have encountered in the process, and finally, to venture a forecast of further development.

Within normal terms of appointment, a head has usually enjoyed powers that can be considered under six broad headings. There is some variation in the extent to which governing bodies have retained control in any of these areas, and there are worrying current tendencies which threaten to take back powers from governors to local councils that I shall refer to later, but whoever holds these six cards is running the school and where governors have trusted the head whom they have appointed, these are the cards that he has been dealt.

First, the head has defined the objectives and the values for his school. He will operate within the limits of what the governors and parents expect, but this is seldom a problem if they have chosen the head they want. (In other words, the constraints will not need to be spelt out as the chosen head will be presumed to have internalised them.) The head seldom needs to make his objectives and values explicit. In fact, part of his power lies in leaving them implicit, or expressed only in ritual, so that they are not exposed to rational cross-examination and consequent modification. They can nevertheless be clearly understood and thus effectively govern the school. Wherever the objectives and values *are* explicit, the head still wins as he is the mouthpiece of the school in all public statement.

Second, the head determines curriculum, what is taught.

Third, distinguished but related, is control of the internal organisation, by which the head has power over access to the courses of learning within the general curriculum. He decides who has opportunity to learn what, who can study German and who has extra woodwork. He controls the timetable. He decides how the pupils are grouped, who teaches them and, within the statutory requirements, how long they stay at school.

Fourth, the head distributes the available money. Therein lies one of his greatest sources of power. He decides how capitation allowances from the local authority are used; he can starve one department to build up another. He virtually controls the distribution of special allowances to the staff, thus having authority over teachers' income outside their basic salaries. In some authorities this distribution of additional payments is made by the governors, but the head's recommendations to them remain crucial. This particular power can become, almost invariably does become, the most resented of all, especially when his distribution of favours remains secret. Through it the head can control staff by promises, threats and bargains. At the same time, he is laid open to promises, threats and bargaining from the lobbying of his staff. It becomes very difficult for a head to be sure when a teacher is being completely honest and frank with him, not saying what he thinks the head wants to hear, and it becomes difficult for the teacher behaving in that way to retain self-respect – which is the main reason for the usual isolation of the head; staff find it easier not to speak to him too often.

Fifth, the head chooses his own staff. The extent to which the local authority qualifies this varies considerably but the head can usually make his pick. In contrast with employees in industry, he cannot dismiss the staff. But my main point is that it is the head who decides for his teachers whom they have to work with. They like his choice or lump it. This was all very well when we only had to tolerate each other in the staff-room and could retreat to the idiosyncrasies of our classrooms, but increasingly now we have to plan and work in close conjunction with these colleagues and feel a growing right to share also in their selection.

Finally, less obvious, but significant, is the degree of power that a head exercises through control of the media of communication. Quite apart from being the spokesman through the external media, via statements to the press, letters to parents, and so on, the head can assert his authority internally by such means as (i) control of paper and print for circulating notices, (ii) convening and chairing staff meetings, (iii) conducting assemblies, (iv) access to public address equipment, (v) installation and distribution of telephones, (vi) preparation of policy statements and reports. All of this amounts to a one-way system of regulative communications, with negligible means of feed-back for assistant staff or students.

At Countesthorpe we have changed all that. The major policy decisions that have shaped the curriculum and discipline of the school have been made by the consensus of the staff. Increasingly, students have contributed to this consensus, and in some instances parents and governors have participated. I accepted the headship in 1972 because I found the policies and the means of determining them attractive, and was prepared to answer for them externally while being accountable internally to the College. I remain as long as those two zones of accountability are compatible. Within the College we have varied executive roles, many of them held interchangeably by staff other than myself and deputies, but without the conventional chain of authority. Our chain of authority links decision-making groups whose composition is not fixed. The body that establishes any ruling consensus is a general meeting, the moot, which is open to all, including nonteaching staff and students. The moot establishes its own constitution, procedures and chairmanship. It meets as necessary, about once in six weeks. Other decision-making groups are responsible directly or indirectly to the moot and any individual may challenge their decisions through the moot.

The sub-groups may be standing or *ad hoc*. The principal standing committee consists of one quarter of the staff with student representation and it holds office for one quarter of the year. Thus every member of staff has a period on committee. Standing committee meets every Monday after school to receive reports and take intermediary decisions. It issues minutes the following day. Other committees include finance committee which is elected annually to make and apply the budget, and *ad hoc* appointment committees set up with each vacancy to select whoever is finally recommended to the authority for appointment to staff. All meetings are advertised and open.

Stated this way, structures appear to dominate. In operation, all depends on the attitudes of the participants, their readiness to use and, if necessary, to modify the structures in order to exercise and take responsibility for powers placed in their hands through them. All six areas of power that I have listed become shared by these means. The moot may finally decide major policy and organisation, but in the preparatory ferment the ideas may spring from any source. Working parties, which eventually formulate proposals for development, are open to all. Anyone may put forward a scheme. It will be tested for its desirability and practicality under the constraints of resources, staffing, space and money. A final proposal will be the work of many hands, a modification of many ideas. Once it is ratified, though, everyone is committed to making it work, because no one has had it imposed from above without opportunity to shape it.

Far from becoming a lift-attendant in a bungalow, the head has much remaining to him. When Countesthorpe opened in 1970, Tim McMullen, its first head, intended to make himself redundant. There are still those who would like to see the head phased out while accepting him as an unfortunate necessity for the time being. I do not share this view and will consider it further in my concluding section. Anyway, what do I do at present?

What I do not do is to allow myself to become the administrator. Except in small schools, where the head may still be a general factotum, heads who allow themselves to become administrators must have a liking for admin. Otherwise they could perfectly well delegate all that square-footage. Most local authorities will appoint someone for that function, responsible to the head. I find that a reliable bursar is indispensable.

For a start, it enables me to remain a teacher (at present I teach a 25 per cent timetable) and a teacher-trainer, in the sense of having an influence upon the practice of less experienced staff. However, this is a role played quite as effectively by a senior teacher, and there is more to my headship than that.

As head, I carry a particular responsibility for continuity. Where the curriculum and organisation unrolls steadily, I need to maintain the diary of events to ensure that the flow is not checked for want of forward planning. I and the deputies (always called 'the executive' for want of a better term by staff) between us attend all meetings. We warn various chairman of deadlines, such as dates for appointments to be made, and initiate working parties before decisions have to be rushed or overtaken by events.

At any meeting, the head's influence is quite unrelated to his voting power. Some critics have expressed disquiet over my having one vote along with any probationer or fifth former. This is beside the point; what one has to consider is what happens before any vote is taken. In that period, the head's influence may take various forms excepting only that it cannot be authoritarian, though it may be authoritative. That is to say, nobody has to accept the wisdom of my view on my say-so : nobody has to do or think what I tell them to because of my position. On the other hand, I do have the authority to give information available to me by right of position, such as rulings from local authorities and legal obligations. And there still remains the possibility of an authoritative (not authoritarian) voice allowed to me by virtue of accorded authority, that is, whatever the others may want to take from me simply because I am me. That authority is a trust that has to be won, can fluctuate and could be lost altogether, but it is real.

If that trust holds, then as head, I have a crucial function as two-way transmitter of pressures. Whether staff want it that way or not, I am the one to whom external authorities refer. Their approaches differ hardly at all from the normal. If the director of education, or any of his many officers or political superiors, want to extract information or commitment from the school, or to communicate either to it, they get on to me. If a parent is unhappy about the school, he identifies it through me. If the press wants a comment, they ring up me. If the chairman of governors wants to pass on a comment, or sound out some proposed move, he buttonholes me. The transmission of pressure is through my bloodstream and I feel no guilt over being paid danger-money.

Perhaps the most important aspect of this osmotic role, is the extent to which I modify actions and decisions in school by sensitising all the participants to outside reaction. There is a regard for my situation, and what might render it an impossible one, going beyond personal consideration (warming though that is when it emerges) to an appreciation of what is possible within the tolerance of public opinion and those in political power. Teachers can remain unusually innocent over political realities lacking, as they do, any continuous face-to-face contact with the adult world. They can usually leave that sort of thing to the head and then denounce his worldliness. At Countesthorpe, though we are not without our Utopians, everyone has been forced to face realities. Their own idealism has been observed in practice (with wildly conflicting reactions), whilst the demands of outside forces have led them to make working compromises in order to survive and prosper.

In so far as this has succeeded – and after every kind of local hostility, we have survived and prospered – it has afforded me a changed kind of satisfaction. Instead of experiencing the gratification of seeing my own educational will take on flesh, as I had done in previous headships, I now feel that I have made possible, and participated in, a form of school in which teachers and school students have been able to enjoy an increase in dignity which results from their sense of determining, to a large extent, the conditions under which they work and grow.

Problems abound. You solve one set only to encounter, and even create, new ones. Some can be surmounted while others remain as permanent constraints. Some I can identify as arising from the role of the head in a participatory government. The problem that most often is raised for me by others is that of possible conflict between head and moot. This is an obvious one only because conflict between head and staff is normal : even under a liberal headship they advise and consent, while he consults and decides. But the participatory system depends upon an initial agreement of aims. That is why it is very doubtful whether an existing school could go over to a participatory approach – I wouldn't recommend it. Countesthorpe was made possible by the first head's clear announcement of intention which enabled him to recruit a staff who wanted to work in that way. With head and staff agreed on basics, then conflicts can be resolved by open discussion in reference to them, provided all parties learn to tolerate conflict, use it to identify issues and make compromises in order to reach consensus. Conflict→compromise→consensus→commitment. Real difficulty arises if we neglect to get together regularly for talk. If this should ever lead to insoluble conflict between me and moot, either I should have to go, or the participatory system would.

A head gets used to just so much talk before he has to make his mind up. Here, the decisions take longer to emerge. This puts a strain upon my tolerance that has made for occasional impatience. In my case the novel situation was made possible by a transitional period between headships as a lecturer at the London Institute of Education. There I learnt to tolerate ambiguity and delayed decision in growing to appreciate the strength of consensus. (I took up smoking, otherwise I think it did me good.) Others it might drive to apoplexy : participatory democracy would not be for them.

Another strain upon my psyche arises from the need to balance the self-effacement of participation with the firmness and fight so often needed on the school's behalf in outside dealings. This alternation of humility with aggressiveness has often required rapid changes of role and I am sure that they have often been confused. Though more obvious in critical times, this probably abides to some degree. One just has to let the problem be known to those who wonder why they have undeservedly been snapped at, and hope they will be understanding.

Of course, some teachers need an authority figure in order to rebel against him. The more mature will have learnt to internalise their enemy, but I have not entirely escaped those who will push one into an authoritarian role apparently in order to object to it. We did have one teacher who boasted that he had taught children to stick pins into headmaster dolls, but he left when the rest of the staff discovered his inflexibility. So we do our best to appoint people who seem to be ready to carry their joint responsibilities.

Turning from the psychological problems to a sociological one, public opinion has a long way to go to catch up with the idea of a head who is anything but autocratic. More than in any other field, people's attitudes to schools are conditioned by the intensive experience of them in the formative period of their earlier years. The head as a stock figure is inevitably anachronistic. Men who have had to learn that negotiation between employer and employee is inescapable have yet to accept that, even if he should want to be autocratic, the head can no longer wield absolute authority, and in the long run will only make himself look ridiculous if he tries to. County councillors who would never risk sacking any of their own employees because they had been on strike may be the very ones who will still demand of a head that he should instruct his staff not to strike. Everyone, from the RSPCA to the anti-abortionists, assumes that if only the head has a word with the pupils in assembly, they will stop it, whatever it is. The only strategy in face of these pious hopes seems to be one of persistence, declaration, and publishing articles like this one.

Of course, power is enjoyable: it enables one to get things done. Even discounting the unreasonable expectations of those who ask for magic from a head, much remains for heads who do not want to relinquish power. I have argued for a spreading of this power, for sharing it with teachers before it is taken into the hands of non-educationists. Nevertheless, it is not a popular argument with heads, and I run a severe risk of antagonising colleagues who see it as undermining their position. I need to reassure them that I do not perceive them all as power-drunk ogres who need to be told their job and deflated into the bargain. Indeed, if they will examine the foregoing they will see that in their own positions, I would be extremely cautious about relinquishing power into dubious hands. How is this paradox going to be resolved?

I do not at present see any maintaining authority entering into contract with a body of teachers on a collegiate basis. Their need to have the accountability of one person ensures the continued existence of the head for some time to come. Given examples of satisfactory stewardship by a head within a participatory system, the most we can hope for is a partnership between LEA and the staff of a school in selection of any new head. A rotating headship is therefore not on, except in non-maintained schools such as those of the Rudolph Steiner foundations.

Parents and teachers should be much less worried over the shift of a head's powers towards his school than over the more sinister threat at the moment of its removal into the hands of non-educationists. His power has at least been checked and balanced up till now by govenors, officers and councillors with a special concern for education. With the establishment of the new enlarged authorities of local government, there has been a detectable pull of power towards their centres. Politicians claiming to act for their electorate have questioned the powers residing with heads and governors, even with education committees, and, in the name of efficient management, have sought to by-pass them. Heads could become accountable direct to councils, and education officers give place to chief executives, civil servants with who knows what notions on education.

Not only does this situation call for vigilance, but it should be borne in mind by those of us trying to spread participatory school government. Any suspicion of irresponsibility on the part of teachers will strengthen the hand of those advocating central authority. Any attempt by teachers to dispense with the head and go it alone would gain no union support at present, and would have no legal basis. The result would only be confrontations that would be destructive to school staffs and damaging to school students. The critical issues therefore are these. Will heads prepare their staffs, students and parents to share more power with them, or will it be removed to the centre? My own guess is that unless heads and teachers work together on this, they will all lose power that will be gathered in to County Hall where the old autocratic head will then sit in all his remoteness under the new guise of efficient corporate management.

16

Some Thoughts on Language and Culture in Schools

MIKE MINCHIN

MIKE MINCHIN was appointed to the original staff at Countes-
thorpe to take charge of the teaching of biology. He has also worked as
a member of one of the teams. Whilst on secondment at Nottingham
University he has been studying the work of Paulo Freire and its sig-
nificance for British schools.

In the course of a much longer study, Mike Minchin argues that
schools traditionally have perpetuated conflict between teacher and
taught. Unless this conflict is resolved, no real learning will occur:
instead, the school will remain an instrument of social domination,
merely training for obedience. Drawing on the ideas of Freire, and
acknowledging the influence of Michael Armstrong's thinking,
Minchin goes on to state that only in a fully democratic setting, where
student autonomy is fostered, can these contradictions be resolved and
alienation avoided.

The following paper has been circulated by Minchin among the staff
with the intention of provoking discussion. In this it has been success-
ful. Staff reactions have varied widely over both his analysis and his
conclusions.

This essay is a modified extract from a longer study I wrote on the con-
text of curriculum, a study which has led me to an interest in the penetrating analysis of language and culture which is presented by Paulo Freire.
As it stands this account is a tentative and derivative attempt to seek
some new ways of looking at what we do with our students in schools.
It draws particularly heavily on two books: *Teaching as a Subversive
Activity,* by Postman and Weingartner and *What School Is For,* by
Chanan and Gilchrist. I have found both these works useful in different
ways, whilst not agreeing entirely with all the assertions made in either of
them. My purpose here is to produce a synthesis which reflects some of the
problems concerned with language and culture which I and several of my
colleagues have faced in our teaching.

It would be a mistake to regard what is written here as an aspect of some 'official' Countesthorpe philosophy. Indeed, I hope that the College will always be a continuously developing place with no time for immutable orthodoxies. The thoughts I express in this account do, however, represent part of my experience of Countesthorpe because new approaches to teaching naturally generate new and different reflections and at Countesthorpe these are taken seriously and not regarded as merely outlandish or seen as appropriate to books but not classrooms. These ideas are, therefore, a contribution to a real dialogue in which reflection is not divorced from action.

It seems sensible to begin with the question: what is the nature of the beings that we teach? Teachers are very much concerned with the development of 'minds' and there is a fascinating array of mind concepts around. R. S. Peters, in his essay 'Education as Initiation', envisages mind first as a product of social development and then as an entirely academic phenomenon. The child, he says, 'learns to name objects, to locate his experiences in a spatio-temporal framework, and to impose causal and means-to-end categories to make sense of events or actions . . .'. Such an embryonic mind is the product of initiation into public traditions enshrined in a public language which it took our remote ancestors centuries to develop. The notion of mind expressed here is amazingly static; no attention is paid to the individual development of language and what is to be learnt is seen as an ancient 'enshrined' set of perceptions. Peters goes on:

'With the mastery of basic skills the door is open to a vaster and more variegated inheritance. Further differentiation develops as the boy becomes initiated more deeply into the distinctive forms of knowledge such as science, history, mathematics, religious and aesthetic appreciation and into the practical types of knowledge involved in moral, prudential and technical forms of thought and action. Such differentiations are alien to the mind of a child and primitive man – indeed to that of pre-seventeenth century man. To have a mind . . . is to have an awareness differentiated in accordance with the canons implicit in all these inherited traditions.'

There are a number of quite astonishing implications here: apparently children, primitive man, all those not directly concerned with academic disciplines, and pre-seventeenth century, man have no minds, or at least no minds worth the name. One is left wondering how most people survive and learn at all, and how the 'enshrined canons' emerged from the mindless sixteenth century. Peters conceives mind as a 'thing', which develops only in terms of the academic disciplines. He confuses the principle of differentiation in thought with the academic form of differentiation. His convictions concerning this must lead him into great difficulties when knowledge is restructured. Presumably when biochemistry emerged from biology it was not real learning, any more than the necessary individual structuring of knowledge is real learning. Such a crude reification of knowledge and education seems to me totally useless to the practising teacher.

It is worthwhile examining the semantics employed in attempts at mental description. Peters and many others represent the mind as an entity which is, therefore, appropriately described by a noun. Most of Peters's assumptions depend upon the qualities inherent in this symbolisation. Yet the mind is not a detectable entity which can be separated from other human attributes. Dewey and Bentley preferred to talk about 'minding', which implies a process, and this process is detectable. Postman and Weingartner similarly choose to view that which is responsible for learning as a process and they talk about 'meaning making'.

The inept use of one noun to describe a particular human attribute leaves the way open for the use of other nouns to describe and separate different aspects of the whole. Thus we have smartness, stupidity, IQ, spirit, emotions, etc. We are led into dichotomies which would be merely puerile if they were not so destructive. Postman and Weingartner in *Teaching as a Subversive Activity* drew attention to the frequency with which such absurd statements as the following are made. 'The school will deal with the child's intellect, the home with his emotions, the church with his spirit' (and, the authors suggest, the hospital with his liver). The verifiable evidence is that people do not function in this way. All functions occur simultaneously.

It is often assumed, or at least educational practice leads us to believe that it must be assumed, that intellect and emotion can be separated. Yet philosophers and psychologists have consistently denied this. Plato said that emotion is important in learning; Vygotsky maintained that it is impossible to form a concept without feeling about it and Dewey talked about 'collateral learning'.

Many of the problems we imagine we are facing in education, low IQs, stupidity and the like, are in truth only grammatical devices with no reality in fact. The semantics we employ are often connotational as opposed to denotational. These things are important because such language enables us to obscure the reality of people. Many teachers talk about strengthening minds, cultivating minds, occupying minds, filling minds or depositing knowledge in minds. Such descriptions, which clearly reflect actions, would not be possible if we abandoned a nounal symbol and the consequent metaphorical extensions. Freire points out that such conceptualisation is dehumanising and McLuhan suggests that the tendency to use nouns as seminal metaphors is a product of print-dominated culture. I am prepared to go farther and speculate that the tendency to reduce people to things is a product of our alienating and dehumanising culture.

What happens when people learn is a process in which their whole being is involved. We need to develop language which will enable us to identify individuals and recognise more clearly their activities which we call learning. I am beginning to doubt the value of this word 'learning' because its existence implies something different from 'living'. If we came to think of what happens in our classrooms in terms of students 'living' in them, we might be less inclined to use inappropriate language in describing our fellow human beings. The teacher who says his job is 'to teach, not wet-nurse the kids' has invented either a special breed of young people or a new kind of life experience. He is as divorced from reality as a university student I met recently who defined the purpose of secondary education as : enabling people to find their level in life. If 'minding' is a process it obviously cannot reach a level until the process stops. The idea of a level is entirely a function of a nounal symbol and a hierarchical social concept. Clearly the symbolic language used provides a ready justification for the fact that people are placed at different social levels. The problem appears to me to be concerned not with the limitation of learning or living but with its appropriateness. The notion of appropriateness involves judgements but it is contradictory to imagine that such judgements can be separate from the learner.

I want now to turn my attention to the question : what happens when someone learns or, as I would call it, lives? Any learning situation is about perception and, in my view, Dewey's notion of transactional psychology remains as one of the most important concepts in education. The idea that perception depends upon a dynamic interaction between what is 'within' and what is 'without' is supported by the experimental work of Adelbert Ames. Postman and Weingartner interpret the most important points made by Ames as follows : perceptions come from us, the nature of reality is perception, there is no other reality. Perceptions are conditioned by experience and purposes; perceptions are unlikely to be changed until their limits are realised by the perceiver. The ability to learn can be interpreted as the ability to relinquish inappropriate perceptions and develop new ones. Each person's perceptions are unique and can only be shared as experience, purposes, etc., are shared. The existence of cultures depends upon public sharing. The nature of perceptions depends to a great degree on the language systems available to the perceiver. Language is the mechanism through which meaning is made and it is only a slight exaggeration to say that we see with our language. The only way we can interpret the meaning of perceptions is through the actions consequent upon them.

These findings and others like them have enormous significance for curriculum.They imply firstly that we must be child-centred simply because there is nowhere else to be. The notion of subject matter beyond people is mythology; there is only individual interpretation of subject matter and the task of the teacher, in this connection, is to develop appropriate shared perceptions of the material. This can only be done if he starts where the student is, rather than where the subject is. Once again, we come back to the notion that education is not, as Peters would have us believe, an act of initiation but rather an act of intervention. A child-centred curriculum implies independent learning; not only are teacher-chosen groups for learning inappropriate to the nature of perceptions but when they involve streaming and setting they introduce expectation factors which have been shown to condition and limit learning.

The abolition of organisational groups will not eliminate the problems that arise from expectation if perceived groups remain. It has been shown that teacher attitude is more important than organisational change. We may interpret this as a teacher perception that children are groupable, as opposed to individual. In my view, one of the most difficult learning problems facing teachers is that of perceiving their classes as individuals. Many pressures exist which incline teachers to think otherwise; pressures arising from their own education, pressures from examinations, pressures from the pseudo-science of much educational testing and overall pressures, both direct and indirect, which stem from the social class structure. Roy Nash in *Classrooms Observed* has shown that in ostensibly unstreamed classes children rapidly learn their position and go on to learn to desire this position. The same must obviously be true of streamed groups and the knowledge that schools prevent learning in this very direct way must surely horrify us all. It is against this background that the vital importance of seeing children as individuals must be considered.

Independent learning is not the same as individualised learning. The assumption, in the most extreme forms of the latter, that children should never learn together seems to me merely ludicrous. Working in groups teaches the sharing of perceptions. The issue is not that class teaching, the sharing of some information or enthusiasm is intrinsically wrong but that it forms the mainstay of our secondary and higher education; and this is wrong. What is in reality only a teaching technique has become elevated to a principle reflecting an erroneous view of learning, and a lack of philosophical sophistication, which is staggering in its proportions. In different circumstances different techniques are appropriate, but obviously the learner must accept the use of a particular method if it is to stand any chance of being effective. We can argue strongly that group co-operation should be encouraged in a society which is so taken up with the idea of competition; but people cannot co-operate without volunteering to do so.

At the centre of Ames's findings is language and it seems to me that schools should conceive their purpose as the teaching of language. Perceptions arise from language and simultaneously language arises from perceptions. The teaching of concepts, which Holly sees as the central purpose, can be interpreted as part of the same process. A concept is a codifying system and perceptions are changed by changes in our codifying processes. I would want in this context to interpret language to be any system of symbolisation that interacts with our perceptions. Thus mathematical symbolisation and scientific symbolisation would be included along with any other relevant language.

The work of McLuhan and others strongly suggests that the nature of language has an important effect in determining the nature of perceptions and that the feedback between language and perception creates a kind of prison for our consciousness. If we are all inevitably imprisoned in this way, how are we to judge whether one form of language is better than another? Presumably not all language is equally good or there would be no need to teach, and what Paulo Freire has called 'cultures of silence' would not exist.

Our decisions in this matter must surely depend upon the relationship between language and action. The test then becomes one of appropriateness or, as Freire has it, 'authenticity'. To put it very crudely and at this risk of being invidious, we might say that language which facilitates learning is appropriate whereas that which inhibits it is inappropriate.

Subjects consist of language systems. Biology is, for example, only that specialised application of symbols that we may call biological language. The same is true of all other disciplines. Yet many educational philosophers appear to conceive of them differently as reified entities which are in some way entirely discontinuous with the language of children and students and must, therefore, be imposed. If we saw the teaching of subjects as the teaching of language we would not isolate that language in a special compartment separate from other language. Our teaching would come to be the sharing of some perceptions and language that we possessed with the student. The nature of the process would be, of necessity, an exchange and its motivation would lie in the fact that the student had found himself incapable of some learning or other action, of which we were capable, by virtue of our different language system.

In more general terms our task as teachers may be seen as the expansion of language and, thus, perceptions. As Wendell Johnson has said 'You can't write writing', not only must you write about something but you must live about something and what we live is what we perceive.

One thing we obviously want students to learn is how to be objective. Probably the most important language skill involved in being objective is that of asking questions. This is hardly taught at all in schools and should be clearly distinguished from guessing answers. The existence of syllabuses, courses and examinations militates strongly against the development of this skill. They all imply the existence of answers and, more importantly, that the way to develop intellectual perception and curiosity is through the study of answers. This is rather like saying the way to learn how to do crossword puzzles is to study the finished article. The notion of courses and syllabuses also implies that the same puzzles are appropriate to everyone.

To take a specific example: biology, some years ago, was taught as an encyclopaedia with experiments demonstrating things that were already known. The advent of Nuffield biology placed the emphasis correctly on discovery but the existence of a course and of an examination, for which over 60 per cent of the marks are awarded for retention, meant that what you were to discover was predetermined and that you then had to remember the answers you got, which had to be the correct answers otherwise they were unexaminable. This is only fractionally more rational than merely learning the answers.

The alternative is to encourage students to ask their own questions and provide them, when the need arises, with the skills and techniques necessary for making progress with the problem. We cannot, of course, assume that at a given moment in time all students will be concerned with biological problems, let alone the same biological problem. This does not remove from the teacher the responsibility for endeavouring to see that all students examine biological phenomena but, in reality, this question should not arise: it is difficult to see how a person could go through school life without ever confronting such a problem. An emphasis on 'question asking' does not mean that there will be no ' "answer" giving'. This can be done through the media of books, films, lectures, etc., but its value is greatly reduced if students do not understand how 'answers' are reached.

It is unfortunate that Postman and Weingartner, in placing correct emphasis on language development, envisage the only way of doing this as through language directly. The lesson examples they quote are all quite high-powered discussions. Such discussions are valuable and are not restricted to 'academic' students, as the example from a remedial group, quoted by Chanan and Gilchrist, shows. To imagine, however, that a school could or should be concerned primarily with such tasks is, in my view, both impossible and wrong.

Their error seems strange because they seem to appreciate fully the relationship between language and·perception. If language must arise from perceptions then, obviously, we can start from there. The provision of new experiences and activities is the provision of new language. We should aim to make the school environment as rich as possible and to encourage language in every possible way but particularly through the medium of talk. It should be remembered that, at present, two-thirds of all talk in classrooms is done by teachers. This is hardly encouraging language development! Schools often say that they are concerned with academic achievement, which can only mean the development of sophisticated systems of language. The assumption that this is best done through the medium of narrative style subject teaching with the aim of passing retention-loaded examinations is to fail to understand the nature of academic inquiry and language.

A consideration of language leads on naturally to a consideration of culture. Most schools would claim to be concerned with culture and many would see their lives bedevilled by what they regard as cultural contradictions. A lot of our thinking about such matters does, however, appear to be far too vague. We frequently hear of 'working-class culture' and 'middle-class culture'. In what sense do these exist? There may be a number of things that derive from the working class and which may be designated cultural, such as dialect, folk song and trade union solidarity. Several of these are, however, now adopted by the middle class. We might immediately think of folk song and an interest in dialect, as well as trade union solidarity amongst several groups of white collar workers. Can we, therefore, continue to refer to these things as aspects of working-class culture if they are shared outside the class? I would contend that we cannot: culture is not something which is passively inherited but something which is re-created and lived. If middle-class people adopt aspects of what was working-class culture, then it becomes their culture. Similarly, a miner who enjoys Beethoven has that music as part of his culture. It seems to be assumed, by some, that cultures exist in opposition to one another, that they, in some sense, answer each other in their different aspects. Thus, we should need to look for a working-class equivalent of Bach in, perhaps, the pub. Obviously culture does not work in this way.

A simplistic idea of middle-class culture is equally misleading. This is often assumed to be synonymous with academic culture but different middle-class groups will, in reality, share very little. The cultural pursuits of an Oxford don are, probably, very different from those of many works managers. Middle-class cultural values such as competitiveness, ambition, prudence, do exist but they are not equally shared within the class, any more than academic culture is; and many of these values have been adopted by the working class.

In education the clash between middle-class and working-class culture, which is assumed to exist, has led to the myth of cultural deprivation. This notion is philosophically unsound because culture is not a commodity but a way of sharing, understanding and celebrating life. It is not something which you can be without; people may be materially deprived but to go on and say they are culturally deprived serves only to rationalise the treatment they have received at the hands of our society. One group may not share the culture of another: many members of the middle class are in this sense deprived of West Indian culture but to speak of overall deprivation is to imply a totally unacceptable value judgement.

Bernstein's work has done much to support deprivation theories of this kind. We may accept the contention that this is really to misunderstand what Bernstein says, or not. The fact is that Bernstein's methods are open to significant criticism and that Labov's results contradict his completely. In schools it is often manifested by practice that working-class language is not worthy of consideration. Teachers assume that the code is restricted and therefore do not hear what is said. A self-fulfilling prophecy is thus created. The practice of penalising language is common in our schools and it is very serious. An individual exists primarily through his language: to reject the language is to reject the individual. Learning is, thus, rendered impossible. Schools which affect to teach middle-class culture are in any case perpetrating a nonsense since it is not the aim of the middle class to recruit the majority of the pupils into its ranks. Working-class students are, therefore, discriminated against both because they are not taught effectively, and because what they are taught is inappropriate.

Chanan and Gilchrist identify five areas of real cultural influence:

working class as such, e.g. trade unionism
regional
popular in the mass media sense
middle-class commercial
academic.

They also develop the very useful notion of pupil culture. Pupil culture will tend to draw on all the other influences but it is most commonly regional, working-class and popular. The culture of pupils is where they are; it is, therefore, valuable to examine the real and apparent nature of the way school culture clashes with pupil culture.

It has been said that the nature of popular culture is that it stimulates a consumer approach to life. Chanan and Gilchrist examine this notion by analysing the development of popular music. They are able to show that there is now much popular music which is of high quality, in both its sounds and its lyrics. More people now play instruments and make their own music; popular music draws on classical European, classical oriental, folk and jazz sources. There is no clash between the established music and the new music. The clash which exists in between commercial interests and musical interests. The major force tending to lower the standards of popular music is the commercial assumptions. A similar analysis to this could be repeated for films, or television.

The importance of this example is that it shows that academic values (which I take to mean appropriate language) do not exist in one place alone. The problem is not to introduce students to the cultural heritage, for they already have such a heritage. Our task is to re-create culture with them and this cannot be done unless we fully acknowledge their autonomy. If the values of formal disciplines have any reality then they must be the same as the values and interests of all people. What is missing in our schools are appropriate reference points and techniques of structuring inquiry.

Eighty-five per cent of our school population do not go on to higher education, and for them the essential problem about schools is that they are not taught very much. For the 15 per cent who do proceed farther the problem lies in the nature of what is taught and the values implied in this. The answer can only lie in a reappraisal of what we do in schools, our school culture. We must resist piecemeal solutions which change none of the basic assumptions, such as the pseudo-progressive notion of a different kind of syllabus for working-class students. This idea, which is closely related to that of cultural deprivation, ignores not only the evidence of Labov but the experience of many practising teachers, who find working-class students as thoughtful and philosophical as any. Appropriate language must be appropriate to all people; relativism is merely a social rationalisation. If this were not so then there ought to be working-class mathematics and science. Working-class children cannot be taught watered-down language because they don't live in a watered-down world. We all live in the same world.

What is at fault is not the nature of intellect or language but the context in which it is presented. Students are exhorted to become mature which means to fit in – as if society is like that. Students must become aware of their real position and of the need for action which will often take the form of resistance and conflict. Working-class students must be helped to realise that they are working class and the question 'what are you going to do about it?' must be raised. Schools are currently greatly concerned with control but control contradicts learning. The development of language must result in actions and these cannot be preconceived or prescribed. The extent to which we do this may be taken as a measure of the extent to which we do not want people to learn.

PART VI

PUBLIC RESPONSE—
POLITICAL REACTION

References have already been made, notably by Virginia Makins and Dr Geoffrey Taylor, to mounting parental anxiety in the first two years. This became a political issue that was kept alive long after the circumstances that gave rise to that anxiety had altered. For those studying innovation in school or other institutions, it will be of interest to note the extent to which a political reaction becomes divorced from the events which prompted it.

In our case, the issue remained alive well beyond the time at which parents had clearly expressed their confidence, for two reasons. The controversial reorganisation of the City of Leicester's secondary schools, following the merger in 1973 of Leicester with Leicestershire and Rutland, caused Countesthorpe, in the words of one councillor, to be 'introduced as an election shuttlecock'. The other reason was that a battle had begun nationally over who should determine what went on inside schools. It is not difficult to see that those who advocated greater external control of schools would have their case strengthened by any apparent need for investigations, let alone by whatever irregularities they might disclose.

In early 1973 a group of disaffected parents gained the support of the local Conservative Member of Parliament, John Farr. His call for an inquiry was then taken up by Councillor Geoffrey Gibson who received full front-page publicity and leader support from the *Leicester Mercury*. The date of 3 April 1973 is significant in that it fell in the week before the major elections to the newly formed council that would be taking control for the first time of the enlarged and much more powerful local government.

Leicester Merc

Incorporating the Leicester Evening Mail

Established 1874   TUESDAY, APRIL 3, 1973

COUNTESTHORPE PROBE ORDERED

THERE is to be a public inquiry, headed by an independent educationalist, into the running of the controversial Countesthorpe College.

The move was announced today by Councillor Geoffrey Gibson, leader of the Conservative group on the County Council, and was given qualified approval by the Labour Party.

Councillor Gibson said: "I recognise parents' concern over Countesthorpe College and we have decided there must be a public inquiry so that everything can be fully examined.

CRITICISM

"An acknowledged authority in education will be invited to act as independent chairman and he will seek the views of parents, staff and of the authority. This is a matter of considerable concern to the public and I am determined that there will be the fullest possible investigation."

Mr. Gordon Parker, on behalf of the Labour Party's new Leicestershire Co-ordinating Committee, commented: 'It seems the Conser-

WE CALLED FOR THIS—

The Leicester Mercury said about Countesthorpe on Saturday:

'The time has surely come when the facts should be established . . . This could best be done by an independent inquiry and the results made known to the Press. Trying to close the doors on this controversy will make it 10 times worse than it already is'.

What we say today—see page 24; Countesthorpe principal on his principles—see page 5.

vatives are sure there is something wrong with the set-up at Countesthorpe College and are quite right in that respect to initiate a public inquiry.

"But if there is something wrong it is criticism of their administraton whch has held sway in the county ever since God made little green apples".

PLEASED

The principal of Countesthorpe College. Mr. John Watts, said he knew nothing of Councillor Gibson's statement.

He added: "Any further inquiries should be made to the Director of Education. We are regularly inspected by Her Majesty's Inspectors of Schools."

Mr. Reg Medhurst, chairman of the college parents' action committee, welcomed the inquiry and said he was "very pleased at the news."

Mr. John Smith, spokesman for the official parents' association, said: "I do not consider that Countesthorpe should become the subject of local party politics

to the detriment of our children's education."

He added that he did not want to make any other comment on the setting-up of a public inquiry "at this stage."

COUN. GEOFFREY GIBSON

A scare a day is Tory tactic —Labour man

TORY tactics in the County Authority elections seemed to be a scare a day, Mr. Gordon Parker said today on behalf of the Labour Party's New Leicestershire Co-ordinating Committee.

He commented: "Their tactics now stand revealed. Complete silence until Labour's pointed questioning flushes them into the open followed by

hastily convened daily press conferences full of sound and fury, signifying nothing.

"Not one word of policy still — just a series of attacks by city Tories on city Labour

Silver stolen in raid on house

BURGLARS walked off with £200 worth of silver when they raided Mr. Frank Petty's house at 118 Station Road, Cropston, yesterday.

They carried it away in a suitcase marked "H.E.P." The haul included a fluted tea-pot with black handles, a matching tea-set, an egg-cooker and bowl and a set of Coronation coins.

On Monday night £10.55 cash was taken from the Advance tapes factory in Abbey Lane.

FIGURE 2

In the period following the elections it was decided that a full inspection would be appropriate means of inquiring into the College. This was mounted in November 1973, three weeks after the 11–13 high school pupils were hived off into their own buildings with their own head who had taken up duties after Easter. We were still suffering from the ravages of the fire, with our administration in huts and our communication routes disrupted. The scars of the abuses and the failures of the building in the first year were still around us. The first wave of sixth formers were heading for A levels.

Enough of the inspectorate report was made known for the local press to make selective quotations. The education committee issued a balanced statement at a press conference.

Then the chairman of the education committee invited parents to meet him and the Director of Education to receive their report. At a packed meeting in the College on 19 June 1974, a summary of the inspectorate report was given. This was the first opportunity also for the principal to address parents on the issue. His report is given here in full. At the end of it there was an overwhelming expression of support by the parents for the directions in which the College was moving.

18

An Address to Parents

by John Watts, Principal of Countesthorpe
College, 19 June 1974

The full inspection of last November has now received comment from
many quarters while I have remained silent. It is time now for me to
speak. However, I do not wish to do so as a penitent. Coming to Countesthorpe as I did only two years ago and seeing the storm clouds already
gathering then, I could have dissociated myself with its beginnings and
called for a new start. Instead, it has been my privilege to identify with
the aims and philosophy of this College, to honour the vision of Tim
McMullen, his courage, his dedication to the good of our sons and
daughters over the decades ahead, and to try my level best to see those
ideas translated into practice. I come therefore to speak not of present
disaster, but of present achievement and an assured future.

I spoke of storm clouds gathering when I arrived. Why were they
gathering? Fundamentally, because so much had been attempted at that
opening in 1970, with insufficient supportive preparation and an un-
precedented amount of publicity. Such a combination proved explosive.
As parents we all have understandable fears and worries for our young.
We want to ensure success for them. Countesthorpe, as it first presented
itself, gave too few of the reassurances that any conscientious parent
needs : more faith was called for than it is fair to expect. The ill-health
of my predecessor added to these fears and reaction began to find expression, at least among a number of parents. The majority? No. The
evidence is there in black and white, that all persons (not all of them
parents) petitioned that they should be given suitable and efficient education for their children under the 1944 Education Act and for freedom
to exercise their right to judge its suitability and their right to freedom of
choice. Quite obviously, some had objections to Countesthorpe in mind,
but it is equally clear that some did not. What is certain is that this statement was given publicity in several quarters which chose to disregard the
reasonable majority of you who put your names, 920 of them, to a state-

ment deploring the effect upon students of the 'sensational publicity to which the school has been subjected' and expressing strong support for the principal and staff in the direction we were taking.

That, you might have thought, would be the end of the matter. But, as a learned judge recently remarked, 'Speculation is the process by which the uninformed reach conclusions'. The issue became a political one, and the cry went up for a full inspection at the time of the election campaign for the new council. This may have been coincidence, but whether it was or not, we suffered for it. The campaign and the inspection and the outcome, which have intruded upon the work of this College for eighteen months now, were based upon a number of very specific queries raised by John Farr, MP. I shall ask you to look again at those charges and ask whether the disturbance they have caused to so many has been justified.

Well, a full inspection was carried out. It was mounted at a time that was educationally inopportune, however politically desirable it may have been. The College had been open for only three years. I had been here only a year. The high school, with its 11–13-aged pupils had been out from under our feet for precisely three weeks, with all the attendant complications of contractors on site, boys and girls moving between buildings in the rainy season, hutted classrooms being towed in and out, cleaning and caretaking concentrating, quite rightly, on getting the Leysland High ready for opening and our sixth form embarking for the first time on their A level year. It must have been an embarrassment to the inspectorate to inspect at such a time, but their orders were to inspect, with all the normal rigours.

And what did they report? I am afraid I am not allowed to tell you. The report is confidential. The staff have added their request for full publication to the secretary of state, so that speculation may cease and the true balance of the whole report may be known. However, it may not be all that necessary now. Our governors and the local education authority have studied the report and made their commentary. Further than that, our local press has, by its own detective work, found out from the report everything it can to our detriment, made it public, and had official confirmation of its *facts* being correct. Its *conclusions* are, of course, another matter, and its headline use of the word 'disaster' has been criticised by the chairman of the education committee. However, we may assume that any of those old charges that could possibly be made to stick have been brought out in the last few days in the press. So I would urge you to read all about it. But *all*. If the report is made public I would urge you to read that, but in its entirety. You will then find that a number of important things emerge.

First, there is an admission that serious errors have occurred. What are these errors, and what has been done about them? Let us be specific. These are errors that I acknowledge:

ERRORS

First and inescapable, excessive damage, particularly in the unsupervised areas, toilets especially.

Second, inadequate materials and finish in certain aspects of the buildings.

Third, as evidenced by that early damage and not entirely excused by flimsy fittings, misbehaviour by students was under inadequate control.

Fourth, the College was opened with an age range 11–14 for which it was not intended, and with boys and girls quite unprepared for the work prepared by teachers in these new surroundings. These pupils included a fair proportion who were within two terms of leaving school, and some of these with no sense of belonging here and, with nothing to lose, caused untold vandalism. Teachers should *never* again be put in the impossible position of having to cope with transfers who are in their last year.

Fifth, we acknowledge that the huge amounts of resource material, including both books and our own internally produced papers, have needed more effective co-ordination and protection.

Sixth, our library was designed in such an open manner that it suffered heavy losses of books until it was removed to an area where it was secure, but inadequately housed.

Seventh, our system of keeping records about students' progress has been too loose, depending too heavily on the knowledge stored in each teacher's memory as a result of the high level of student–teacher contact. But also, *Eighth*, insufficient time had been allowed for staff to prepare the administrative machinery necessary for running the school on the lines intended.

Ninth, and summing it up, too many innovations may have been introduced at once, with the important corollary that *Tenth*, insufficient time had been allowed to prepare the ground for them.

Those are my ten admissions of error. Let us indeed hope that they will never be repeated. You have been told that they have been put right or are in the process of being put right. In case that sounds too bland, may I again be specific about our remedial action to date.

REMEDIES

First, damage. The damage rate is now down to the minimum that any comparable school may hope for. Staff duties are now so arranged that all areas are given more specific attention. Repairs and redecorations due to us are now in hand.

Second, inadequate fittings are gradually being repaired.

Third, attitudes towards behaviour and care of our surroundings have changed considerably as staff have developed a consistent approach to the subject and pursued the matter with students, who in turn have a sense of belonging and responsibility that could not have been found in those opening days.

Fourth, from being 11–14, we have this year become 14–18. Never again will our biggest and oldest be the most disaffected and unruly.

Fifth, we have appointed an experienced and senior teacher to organise, co-ordinate and develop our resources.

Sixth, in conjunction with this, the director has arranged for the original library area to be panelled in so that it may be secure enough for its intended use by the start of next term.

Seventh, a complete survey of our system has been embarked upon so as to bring record-keeping to a more satisfactory level.

This much will, I hope, indicate that on staff we have made a professional response to the full inspection. Untimely as this full inspection was, the discussions with the various subject HMIS were constructive and stimulating.

But let us pause and ask again whether these were the issues over which we were hammered and harassed last year. Are these the errors that our critics were so anxious to have proved? Do they bear any relationship to John Farr's much publicised ten points, and what has become of them? What were the charges? Which had substance and which should now be withdrawn?

I feel obliged to recall those charges and although I am not free to refer to the report of the inspectorate, I can, thanks to the local press, refer to what it has revealed. You may well guess that anything to our discredit in that report has by now found its way into their columns, and even some of those things to our credit appear from time to time in the small print. In the following list I can only refer to the reportage of the local press. Were the official report not confidential, I could quote much more fully on what has been said to our credit.

1 *Charge*: The staff are not up to quality.
   Comment: Press quote – 'The Inspectors' report had come out in warm praise of several aspects . . .', 'Staff are commended for their dedication to students' welfare and the warmth and trust of their relationships'.

2 *Charge*: Basic subjects are neglected, particularly English, maths, religious education.
   Comment: Press quote – reference was made to 'very good standards being achieved in some subjects and the promise [that was] apparent in most of the others'. Even though RE is specifically mentioned on 14 June 1974 in the press quotes, there was no indication that the inspectorate are not satisfied with its provision.

3 *Charge*: The teachers were indoctrinating students with left-wing opinions, using biased material.
Comment: Press quote – 'There was no evidence found of any political bias in teaching'.

4 *Charge*: Students suffered from lack of regular homework.
Comment: No mention made, so we may assume that the inspectorate have not confirmed this.

5 *Charge*: Sex instruction given is offensive to parents.
Comment: No mention made, so we may assume that the inspectorate found no cause for concern.

6 *Charge*: X films are shown against parental wishes.
Comment: The inspectorate are reported as saying that parental consent in writing is obtained before any student sees an X film. (Note: for many, X film seems to mean Sex film.) The inspectorate disapproved of our showing the film *War Games*, as it was horrific.

7 *Charge*: Staff have little interest in exams, indeed some said we intended abandoning exams.
Comment: Press comment – 'Overall results were like the curate's egg – good in parts and bad in others'. (A devastating revelation?)

8 *Charge*: Leavers would have difficulty in finding anyone to employ them.
Comment: I can verify that to date all our leavers have gone into employment.

9 *Charge*: Students are absent to a high degree and arrive late.
Comment: Press quote – 'The Education Committee would not consider attendance figures excellent – nor diabolical'. Late arrival is still a cause of concern for us on staff.

10 *Charge*: Unrestrained violence was frequent.
Comment: In an age where violence is not uncommon in schools and out, you might think evidence would be easy to find. None is reported.

11 *Charge*: Students are at a disadvantage from lack of a uniform.
Comment: No comment from the inspectorate is noted, which is not surprising.

12 *Charge*: That theft was rife at the College.
Comment: No evidence is reported, so we may assume the inspectorate found none.

13 *Charge*: That the running of the school was in the hands of a sinister power group.
Comment: No suggestion of such splits. The report as quoted in the press suggests a uniformity of staff commitment to what they are doing.

14 *Charge*: The College disregarded parents' wishes and the community.
Comment: The inspectorate have not confirmed this in any way, and hardly need to since we have had a signed statement of confidence from our parents.

15 *Charge*: Our educational philosophy of aims is contrary to approved notions.

    Comment: Had the inspectorate taken issue in any way with our fully stated principles of educational thinking and method you may be sure they would have said so and been reported in full. There is no mention of such disagreement.

Bearing in mind even those errors admitted, does not this awful charge sheet look thin? So thin that one wonders whether such disruption of everyone's work for nearly two years has been warranted.

The press also refers again to the paper entitled 'Fact and Fiction' that I sent to you all in April 1973 in an attempt then to lay some of the myths and distortions going the rounds. It was a closely packed statement with many details of fact. The press now reports that the inspectorate scrutinised that document and I am sure that if anything in the slightest bit dubious had been noted by them, the press would have reported it. What do we hear? Were my claims disputed on curriculum, or my exam statistics, my answers on discipline or on teaching competence? It would seem not. It would seem that the only comment is that I claimed that we do not tolerate anti-social behaviour whereas anti-social behaviour has been observed. This is like saying that the Church does not tolerate sin, yet sinning continues, or that the Law forbids crime, yet crimes continue. You may disbelieve that HM inspectorate could offer this as serious comment, yet the press says they did, and officially we hear that their facts are correct. And that is the extent to which 'Fact and Fiction' was faulted under such close examination.

Now let us turn again to the present and future. The press and the local education authority have recognised 'certain positive and valuable achievements' at the College. Let me be specific again and ask what these are, and whether even in the small print of the press there is any reference to what the inspectorate said. I could add to this the main features that have aroused the interest and praise of schools and teachers elsewhere in the country and from all round the world.

ACHIEVEMENTS

(i) There is, for a start, the individualised approach to learning, with its hand-tailoring of each student's timetabling. (This applies in all subjects, but in science, for instance, it has led to the formation, by Eric Green, head of physical sciences, of a national movement – Independent Learning in Science, helped by the Inspectorate and our local education authority.)

(ii) The development of a team-based approach to the core curriculum which unites, under the same teacher, the pastoral care of each student with the main subject teaching. This is undoubtedly bringing about 'the more ordered and stable organisation' that has been asked for. Mark, it has been asked for up and down the country, especially since the school-leaving age was raised this year, and others visiting us have not been slow to seize upon this as one of the 'approaches to learning and teaching likely to contribute valuably to the fund of educational knowledge' noted by our local education authority.

(iii) Our inquiry-based curriculum and the opportunities for students to participate with staff in making the decisions that affect the working conditions within the school are leading them into a better practical understanding of what is entailed in negotiating, entering into a contract and honouring it, reasoning and listening (characteristics surely needed in the adults of the next generation as well as this).

(iv) In fact, I would claim that we are implementing what others have for long been demanding, a new deal in comprehensive secondary education following the raising of the school-leaving age, for the age-group 14 to 18. It is a deal no longer based on ultimate sanctions or threats, or the bluff that these can still apply at this age-level. It is a deal based on new relationships that recognise that students arrive here at the age at which most of the adult population *left* school to earn a wage, and that our upper age-range is one to which we have as a nation given the vote, and for a long time the opportunity of joining up and giving life in our defence.

THE FUTURE

You have had assurances that errors will not be repeated. Teachers, too, will applaud this. But does this mean that the future will be free from problems? Far from it. All schools are moving, with the rest of us, into unknown futures. No one wants their offspring experimented with irresponsibly. But from the moment of birth, all of a child's future is hazardous. Shirley Williams remarked last week : 'There are hazards in anything one does, but there are greater hazards in doing nothing at all.' I would add that the most irresponsible educational experiment would be standing still and pretending that what was good for schools in the past, however recent, will be good for them now and henceforth.

All innovation has suffered the fires of derision, hostility and disbelief. Galileo, you may remember, could not persuade some of his professors that the earth went round the sun rather than the reverse, because they refused to look down his telescope for fear that what they would see might prove him right.

My confidence in the future at Countesthorpe rests on the following :

(i) Errors have been remedied or are being remedied. Damage is being restored and has ceased to occur on those earlier levels. What has been restored, like the areas around the burnt-out offices, has, after three months use, remained in perfect condition.

(ii) The library and resource provision will have new co-ordination and new secure areas.

(iii) Our student age-level has risen from its original 11–14 to the intended 14–18 and correspondingly mature attitudes have developed. The participation in school affairs has led to staff–student relationships that enable us to work by reason and agreement. (Evidence of this is shown by the remarkable good sense and maturity with which students accepted that this meeting should be closed to them, even after I had, through my own blunder of hasty invitation, led them to think they would be welcome. They could very rightly have been highly indignant, considering the responsible way in which they have come to open meetings as a matter of course now, but they wished to avoid the College any further embarrassment. Their decision shows a degree of understanding and responsibility from which we their elders might learn.)

(iv) I am encouraged by the extent to which other teachers and other schools are moving in the same general direction as we are at Countesthorpe.

(v) I am encouraged by the fact that whatever else the press has gleaned from the report on the school, they have reported no fundamental point in our philosophy with which HM Inspectorate take issue, for had they done so, you may be sure it would have been given prominence.

(vi) Finally, I take greatest heart from the support and confidence expressed in us by the parents, formally over a year ago, but confirmed by every comment since, and now more recently by our governors and the education authority.

I will only add my personal thanks for support over this intensely stressful period to the students and staff, without whose backing the whole venture would have been impossible, to the PTA, to the officers of the LEA, and in particular to Dr Geoffrey Taylor, chairman of the governors, whose advice, encouragement and good humour have enabled me to keep my head up and my feet on the ground.

It may be of interest to note the contrast of headings given to press reports of that meeting.

The *Leicester Mercury*, putting the matter perhaps in the context of its own earlier demands for an inquiry, on 20 June 1974, stated:

COLLEGE WARDEN ADMITS ERRORS WERE MADE

The *Guardian*, looking from a little farther away, reported on 21 June 1974:

PARENTS SUPPORT SCHOOL STAFF

That was not the end of the matter, however. The Leicestershire Education Committee set up a special sub-committee to consider the Inspectorate's report, receive evidence from parents, governors and any others it might wish to consult and to report with recommendations. Under the chairmanship of Councillor John Rodgers, the special sub-committee deliberated for most of the school year, actually came to the College for an hour one afternoon, and reported eventually in the summer.

In spite of staff objection to a number of errors of fact and implications in the report, it was submitted to the education committee for its meeting on 1 July 1975. Although anxious that the education committee should finally give its approval to our work, we were even more concerned to win this under no false pretences. Many of those who had watched us, for one reason or another, had been known to say that under the pressure of the preceding three years, we had retracted on major points of principle. We therefore stuck our necks out and issued the following statement to all members of the education committee.

19

Statement to the Education Committee

By the Staff – Student Standing Committee,
1 July 1975

To: The Chairman and Members of the Education Committee
From: The Members of Countesthorpe College

1 July 1975

The report prepared by the special sub-committee
of the schools committee on Countesthorpe College

The most significant passage in the report is the statement 9.8. 'that Governors and most parents have expressed unreserved confidence in the direction and work of the Principal and Staff'. This was public knowledge over a year ago, before the special sub-committee was ever set up. All that the report has done therefore is to come up with rehashed information and opinions that are neither consistent nor adequately substantiated.

The recommendations and the timing of the report, coupled with the response made to it already in the local press, strongly suggest that it is an exercise in local politics. We deplore the manner in which the College, by the equivocal tone of the report, is once more made a subject of speculation. It can in no way be considered as a full or fair summary of the College's development over its first five years, arising as it does out of events predating our arrival at the point of being 14–18 upper school that we were planned to be and now are. It fails to specify either our real problems and mistakes or our aspirations and very real achievements.

In its opening phase, this College had grave problems, many of which were far from our own making. This at least the report does mention. Mistakes were made and lessons learnt, as was reported in some detail to parents by the principal twelve months ago. Nevertheless, our aims and philosophy, clearly announced since the opening, and reiterated at the time of the inspection in 1973, have remained unchallenged. They represent an approach to popular schooling, including the two years now compulsory from 14 to 16, which is based upon contract rather than upon coercion. They entail a system of operation by agreement rather than by command, and this system extends to the staff and principal as well as the students.

In practice it was found that once the school reached its intended status, with 14–18-year-olds, the dividends were being paid. Without sacrifice of examination results, university and college entries or employment prospects, relationships of unusual trust have been established between teachers and students. The school is virtually free of violence and threat of violence, at a time when violence is a widespread social problem.

Reference to our 'team' system indicates a failure on the part of the sub-committee to understand its complexity and its achievements. In particular, the report overlooks these features: (1) the teams are fully comprehensive in membership, whereas specialist groups may be less than fully so; (2) the staff–student relationships have decisively reduced damage to premises and eliminated violence; (3) examination results in subjects covered within teams have included our best (the indications are that at least one-third of our total intake will this year obtain two O level passes from the work undertaken in team time alone); (4) the team approach, uniting the teacher's pastoral care with the teaching of core subjects, is an innovation that has aroused interest from other schools at home and abroad, many of whom are adapting the system to their own use.

Furthermore, over internal organisation, while the principal's ultimate contractual responsibility to the governors and local education authority is fully recognised, our capacity to find consensus and shared commitment through the workings of the moot means that it has not been found necessary to alter our basic procedures whereby the moot and the community council formulate the College's policy with the full co-operation of the principal who, with his deputies, carries the executive responsibility.

To have come so far in five years is an achievement of which we are proud. Recognition has been accorded by the educational world; confidence has been expressed by parents and governors; it is timely that the education committee should endorse that recognition and support.

This school, like any other, has always been responsive to the advice of Her Majesty's Inspectorate and the advisers of the local authority. We view with disquiet the production of this report by a lay body and its suggestion of a county inspectorate. We expect that note of this new departure will be taken by the Department of Education and Science, and by teachers' representative bodies.

The report rakes up the past unnecessarily at a time when our new intake of students is preparing for transfer. They need the smooth transition which had been carefully organised in co-operation with our contributory high schools. Instead, this raising of old worries is bound to be unsettling for them, their parents and their teachers. It is time now for the education committee and the county council to condemn any further harassment of this College along with their expression of that support already given by governors, parents and the overwhelming majority of those who have visited us at our work.

On behalf of the staff and students
of Countesthorpe College

Dennis Roberts	Chairman of Standing Committee
John Watts	Principal

[The education committee met on 2 July to receive the report commissioned a year earlier from its schools committee. Having discussed it, the committee gave the requested vote of confidence in, support for and encouragement of the principal, staff and governors.]

PART VII
WHERE WE DIFFER

20

An Exchange of Letters

Between Michael Armstrong and Professor
G. H. Bancock

G. H. BANTOCK was Professor of Education at the University of Leicester School of Education. He has been an important figure in discussions of popular education, being best known perhaps by his Freedom and Authority in Education *(Faber, 1965), and more recently as a Black Paper contributor. Although Professor Bantock has not visited Countesthorpe College, he has taken a keen interest in its development and has from time to time made comment on it as reported by his colleague Professor Gerald Bernbaum in his study of 1971. It was after one such comment in 1975 that Michael Armstrong felt prompted to write to Professor Bantock. There followed a lengthy correspondence of a highly unusual nature. It is instructive and revealing to those who will follow the argument through, and we are grateful to both the correspondents for their permission to publish.*

18 April 1975

Dear Professor Bantock,

As a former pupil and acquaintance, who has long respected your writings while frequently rejecting their arguments, I have been encouraged by friends and colleagues at Countesthorpe to write to you to express our concern over what we feel to be a misinterpretation of our principles and of our practices to be found in a number of your recent writings and public statements about 'progressive' education. I am thinking especially of your esays in the forthcoming Black Paper and in *A Question of Schooling*, ed. John Macbeath, to be published next year, as well as of remarks which, as we understand from John Hipkin, you made during a recent recording for Thames Television. In each case you would seem to have implied that it is our policy and practice at Countesthorpe to abandon 'academic' goals in favour of other ends and purposes, or at any rate relegate them to a relatively lowly place in the order of educational priorities, citing as evidence in support of your implication the study by Gerald Bernbaum published by OECD in 1973.

Now in the first place I am rather surprised that you should have considered Bernbaum's study to offer convincing evidence of our present intentions or achievements. Not only is the study, on Bernbaum's own admission, 'of only a tentative nature', but it was conducted within a very few months of the opening of the school. We are now in our sixth year and inevitably Bernbaum's observations have been overtaken by events. I would have expected you, in the interests of accuracy, to have tried to discover at first hand something about our present aspirations. After all, you live and work nearby, and our own contacts with the School of Education are frequent and close. One of your colleages works here half-time while one of your fellow professors is on our governing body. I myself am at least known to you and would have been only too glad to talk things over with you.

I doubt, in any case, if Bernbaum's evidence is capable of supporting your apparent interpretation, or even, for that matter, the interpretation he offers himself. You cite his evidence that 'when the teachers were given a list of 12 items by means of which the influence of the school would make itself felt and asked to say whether the item was likely to be "Highly Important", "Moderately Important", or "Not Important" the two items which received the highest number of "Highly Important" rulings were (1) Visible improvements in pupils' social adjustment, (2) Visible inprovements in the community's involvement in the school, [while] visible improvement in pupils' academic achievement was placed eleventh out of twelve in the "Highly Important" column'. Bernbaum's assumption that this 'finding' tends to confirm his suspicion that teachers at Countesthorpe 'are interested in the expressive features of their work rather than in the cognitive and instrumental aspects of it' is, to say the least, tendentious. (Incidentally have you noticed how, throughout his study, Bernbaum systematically confuses the terms 'cognitive' and 'instrumental', as indeed I suspect you are in danger of doing yourself, to judge from the draft I have read of your essay 'A Question of Quality'.)

The actual question teachers were asked was this: 'Many people see Countesthorpe as the school of the future and as being influential in bringing about changes in educational organisations. Do you agree with this view? . . . If yes, by what means do you see the influence of the school making itself felt?'

All the answers can mean then, if indeed it is imaginable that such a ramshackle question might produce meaningful answers of any kind, is that most teachers assumed that visible improvements in pupils' academic achievement would not be a highly important means of making the influence of the school felt in helping to bring about change in educational organisations. To deduce from this that the teachers considered academic achievement to be unimportant either as an end in itself or even as an instrumental goal is a piece of illogicality which is truly worthy of educational sociology. I do indeed remember, while attempting to answer Bernbaum's questionnaire myself, how I could not help reflecting over and over again on the impossibility of providing reasonable answers to such exasperating and inadequate questions. I am astonished to find you accepting this evidence at face value, knowing from my student days your justifiable distaste for such primitive and misleading techniques of inquiry.

In a way, though, this is all beside the point. I would argue that, had Bernbaum returned to the staff on the completion of his research and asked them whether they considered 'academic' achievement or 'academic' values to be relatively unimportant, very few would have concurred. But than can no longer be tested. What can be tested is the way the staff feel today. I think I can reassure you that you would be hard put to find a single teacher here who wished to devalue 'academic' achievement and I would be delighted to demonstrate this to anyone who should happen to doubt it.

There are perhaps two ways in which you might try to secure your argument, despite any reassurance I can offer in respect of our present intentions. First, you might argue that the effect, if not the intention, of our policies is in practice to devalue academic goals and pursuits. Undoubtedly Bernbaum's study shows that he himself believed this to be a risk the school would inevitably run. For myself, I do not accept Bernbaum's analysis of the nature of the risk involved, nor do I believe that in the event academic goals and pursuits have been devalued in consequence of our policies. Nevertheless there are those among our critics, including critics who are in general sympathetic to our goals, who would argue that we do indeed run some such risk and I would accept that this is still at least a matter for dispute. But I cannot see how the risk of something happening justifies you in asserting that it has already happened. As far as I can see you have offered no evidence to support such a contention, as far as Countesthorpe is concerned, and the 'evidence' presented by Bernbaum in his study is, to be charitable, inadequate to sustain his conclusion, however tentative.

Or you might argue that we hold different notions of what is to count as 'academic achievement' from those of a more traditional school, for example than those of Highbury Grove under Rhodes Boyson. So we do. For one thing we believe that the traditional school too often succumbs to the temptation to identify academic standards with examination successes, or learning with competing. Bernbaum's confusion of 'cognitive' and 'instrumental' suggests that he is himself a victim of this identification, and I find it interesting to observe that you also, in 'A Question of Quality', appear to equate the 'high academic reputation' and aim of Highbury Grove with Dr Boyson's emphasis on 'the instrumental role of the school'. (Could there be a more striking illustration of that tendency, for which you berate what you call 'the radical left', to 'see knowledge exclusively as a means of control and not as a means of release, or of an extension of powers'?) More positively, we argue that a 'progressive' approach to teaching and learning – as you say, 'the purpose of schooling is learning' – is certain in due course to transform our understanding of the nature of academic values, an argument which, I would readily admit, is easy to assert but hard to demonstrate. (I have begun a personal attempt to demonstrate the argument in a couple of articles in the current issue of *Forum* and I am sending you a copy.) But whatever the outcome of an argument concerning the nature of academic values it cannot reasonably be presented as an argument between those who are committed to and those who are indifferent to those values.

In sum, it is wrong to imply that teachers at Countesthorpe are less concerned with 'academic achievement' than with 'social attitudes'; wholly false to conclude that our intention is to devalue academic purposes and probably false to suggest that such is the effect if not the intention of our policy and practice. On the other hand it is certainly true to say that we reject the dichotomies between academic concern and pastoral care or between instrumental and expressive roles or between cognitive and affective realms or even, indeed especially, between the 'voice of dynamic sound' and the 'words of understanding', as systematically misleading and therefore intellectually corrupt. We accept the goal of 'a democracy of shared meanings' and the definition of opportunity in terms of equality of 'access to forms of knowledge, modes of perception, ways of thinking – in short to varieties of reality' as opposed to equality simply of 'access to educational institutional institutions'. To describe this goal as 'homogenis-ation in terms of culture, achievement, experience' or even as 'equality of outcome' is to misconstrue it, to ignore the richness of variety which is compatible with, is indeed entailed by, a universe of shared meanings, while to say that the goal is unattainable because 'for whatever reason – original endowment or social upbringing in the family – the ability to grasp meaning varies ineluctably from child to child in a way that no social engineering can erode' is to assert the unprovable in the face of innumer-able counter examples. It is more realistic as well as more hopeful to ex-plore the ways in which the structures of popular education (at the level of curriculum, method, discipline and professional and personal relation-ships just as much as at the level of organisation) have inhibited if not repressed the growth of intellect and to search for more productive alternatives. What is happening at Countesthorpe, quite simply, represents one attempt to find some such alternative.

I would like to be able to go on now to describe our intentions in more detail but I am conscious that this letter is already inordinately long and the task of description might demand as much as a small book in itself. Instead I am sending you a copy of the two articles I wrote recently for

Forum and three documents concerning the development of some of our ideas at Countesthorpe. I hope that these may give you some idea of the overall pattern of our thought.

Meanwhile I must thank you for once again goading and challenging my own thinking. I send you my very best wishes and I hope that sometime we may meet each other again.

Yours very sincerely,
Michael Armstrong

23 April 1975

Dear Mr Armstrong,

Many thanks for your letter of 18 April. I was glad to hear from you after such a long interval.

Let me begin by making it quite clear that, in quoting from the Bernbaum article in several pieces of my own, my intention was not to 'knock' Countesthorpe College. It simply happened that this particular article provided me with some hard evidence in order to illustrate something which undoubtedly does characterise a number of our comprehensive schools. My point is that the comprehensive school often lacks a defined ethos, and that this springs from a certain polarisation of staff attitudes to the *relative* importance of academic learning. You may criticise Professor Bernbaum's article; I can only say that I find him, after consultation, unrepentant. (He has seen your letter.) And he informs me that the article was submitted to Mr McMullen for comment and criticism before it was published. Furthermore, I did make inquiries from colleagues concerning any recent developments – hence a footnote that appears on page 18 of my Black Paper article.

Reading your letter carefully, it seems to me that, in a sense, the second half more or less admits that there is a case to be answered – a fact that the first half clearly wants to rebut. You refer to the fact that you have critics sympathetic to your goals who would argue that you do run the sort of risks to which I am referring, and you accept 'this is still at least a matter for dispute'. Secondly, of course, you admit that it may be that we differ as to what counts as academic achievement, and this I think is probably true. Underlying the conflict of fact I think there is undoubtedly a conflict of values.

My point, then, is not that Countesthorpe, as presented in Bernbaum's paper, repudiates academic values, but simply that it presents a blurred image of what it is about. I make the point, which Bernbaum also makes, that 'the graduate teachers tend to emphasise academic goals and the nongraduate opt for relationships and socialisation'. Furthermore, I feel that at least some of the documents that you have sent to me only tend to confirm the fact that academic values in the sense in which I hold them would be at some risk at Countesthorpe. (Incidentally, I have never claimed that results have been' poor – as you know there is no public information about this – I simply claim that they are at risk.) It is quite clear from your crucial Document 1, for instance, that the curriculum is intended to be largely student-centred, and that 'relevance', narrowly concerned, is a primary aim. This, in fact, is just what I have to say about the implications of socialisation in terms of curriculum content – the main purpose of my Black Paper article. Indeed there is a constant confusion in this document, as I see it, between concern for the logical and psychological aspects of learning. One of the putative advantages, for instance, of your 'model' is thought to be reflected in the statement: 'It offers students a range of learning activities less strictly subject-centred and a greater freedom to vary their programme of work from day to day and from week to week. For instance, a student totally uninvolved in mathematics can stop doing it altogether for a time, while the maths teacher within his core group watches and waits for signs of involvement which he might turn to mathematical effect.' What, I wonder, happens if such a teacher never notices any such involvement, or if the student refuses to accept the teacher's efforts to use such signs for mathematical effect? My wife teaches remedial reading in a primary school. If she adopted your policy some of her charges would never learn to read – and this would be a great deprivation for them. As Lawrence said, we must accept responsibility for our children. (You can argue that maths is only suitable for some children up to a certain standard – but then it must be replaced by something else, more educative for *them* but *insisted* on.)

Another point: I do not think there is any necessary division between academic standards and examination success. In my *Industrial Society* I did criticise examinations; but in recent years I have come to think them increasingly necessary both for teacher and pupil, on the grounds that, firstly, examinations are not necessarily bad in themselves, though a number of them display weaknesses in the sort of questions that they deploy. Our attention, indeed, should not be directed *against* examinations but *towards* improving them. Secondly, in an imperfect world it seems to me we often have to accept the not quite so good in order to avoid a situation which is even worse. And I have become increasingly convinced of the need for (well-constructed) tests as a necessary part of the educational scene. No doubt we shall fail to agree here.

I think perhaps, however, the key to our disagreement will come over your statement that you 'reject the dichotomy between academic concern and pastoral care, and between instrumental and cognitive and affective realms', etc. As members of the Black Paper have insisted, and as I myself point out in my introduction to my *Education, Culture and the Emotions,* one of the marks of a certain type of progressive thinking of our times is this dislike of making discriminations and distinctions. I clearly recognise a distinction between, for instance, academic concern and pastoral care as those terms are normally used. Furthermore, although the distinction between affective and cognitive, where school subjects are concerned, exists on a continuum, it is idle to argue, in my view, that the cognitive content of a mathematical formula or a statement of a scientific proof does not occupy a different place on the continuum from, shall we say, a poem or a work of art. And I don't think we get anywhere by failing to accept divisions which can be objectively pointed to. Again you state 'We accept the goal of "democracy of shared meanings" and the definition of how, in terms of equality, access to forms of knowledge, codes of perception, ways of thinking – in short, to varieties of reality' as opposed to equality simply of 'access to educational institutions'. Precisely, and this, I think, is where you go wrong. We can't, I think, even ensure equality of access to educational institutions. But as the whole of my article is intended to imply, a democracy of shared meanings can only be brought about within a totalitarian society. 'The fool sees not the same tree that the wise man sees', as Blake put it, and, as I say, Blake is hardly an Establishment figure. So how can it *mean* the same to both of them? There are certain varieties of reality which are open to some and will for ever remain closed to others. My evidence for this is simply the whole of human history which continually demonstrates the wide variety of intellectual and cultural grasp which characterises different sections of the community. (St Thomas Aquinas and the mediaeval peasant did not worship the same God – one worshipped an image, the other a highly intellectually conceptualised realisation of the God-head.) But you can retort that I can't *prove* this. Of course I cannot prove it in the trivial sense that no one can predict what will happen tomorrow; but the weight of probability is immeasurably on my side.

Well you, too, have stimulated me to try to explain myself more fully. I only wish that all my opponents argued with me as courteously as you have done. I suspect at the end of the day we must simply agree to differ, but you have admitted that I have got you challenging your own thinking, and this is what I see to be the function of the Black Papers. You will note, too, that I indicate that I know the schools are in a genuine dilemma. I have, as you know, my own suggestion for coping with it (cf. my article 'Towards a Theory of Popular Education' in *The Curriculum*, ed. R. Hooper for Open University).

You probably know that I am retiring at the end of this term and wish to devote myself more to writing. I am going to concern myself with a history of educational thought from the time of the Renaissance to the present day. This is something I have long wanted to accomplish, but the continual day-to-day administrative demands of my present job have made it impossible for me to give my whole-hearted attention to such an undertaking.

All good wishes.

Yours sincerely,
G. H. Bantock
Professor of Education

30 April 1975

Dear Professor Bantock,

Thank you so much for your patient and interesting reply to my letter. I hope you will forgive me if I return just one more time to the nature and cause of our dispute. Perhaps in the end, as you say, we have to agree to differ. But at the risk of appearing somewhat shrill or insistent, I would like to clarify my position a little further in the light of your reply, if only to feel more certain that we have understood each other's position.

The credibility of Professor Bernbaum's study seems to me now a relatively minor point of disagreement. All I can usefully add to your comment is that, notwithstanding Bernbaum's reluctance to repent, I would still wish to argue that the Countesthorpe pictured in his essay is rather a poor likeness. Unfortunately the form of the essay makes it impossible to arrive at an objective judgement of the matter since Bernbaum presents virtually none of the raw data on which his interpretations depend. You stress his point that it's the graduate teachers at Countesthorpe who tend to emphasise academic goals while the non-graduates opt for socialisation. It might then be of some significance to note that since 1973, when the schools became exclusively an upper school as originally intended, three-quarters of the staff have been graduates. I would also guess, with some confidence although I haven't the precise figures to hand, that in 1970, when there was a somewhat larger percentage of non-graduates on the staff, most of them taught the so-called non-academic subjects, so that any divergence between theirs and the graduate teachers' views might well be a good deal less revealing that Bernbaum imagines. Incidentally this possibility surely demonstrates the difficulty of assessing Bernbaum's interpretations without access to more data.

But enough of Professor Bernbaum's study, there are more urgent matters between us. First a point of interpretation. You say that it is clear from the first document I enclosed that 'the curriculum is intended to be largely student-centred and that "relevance" narrowly concerned, is a primary aim'. Certainly our curriculum is intended to be student-centred inasmuch as each student is offered a large measure of autonomy in the determination of his own curriculum with the help and guidance of his teachers (remember, incidentally, that our youngest students are already 14). But I don't quite agree that 'relevance', narrowly concerned, is a primary aim. 'Relevance' for us is not so much an aim as a point of departure. I quoted in that document from an essay by John Dixon which puts it nicely, I think, in relation to the teaching of English. We begin with that 'area of experience which can and does reflect (directly or meta-phorically) things of importance to an individual, first within the narrow circle of home and neighbourhood, and progressively in widening circles of the world as he comes to grips with it. The English teacher, and the school at large, has to try to widen that circle by stimulating a curiosity about what lies beyond such that a pupil actively extends his immediate concerns.'

It is the responsibility of the teacher to introduce into this widening circle whatever he judges will promote a concern for, and a commitment to, the major disciplines of human thought (mathematics, science, the humanities, the arts). As I understand it, you argue that no teacher can hope to do this without imposing on his pupils a very substantial measure of compulsion. Hence your conviction that academic values are bound to be at some risk at Countesthorpe.

If I may briefly digress here, I notice that you attribute our failure to recognise the necessity of compulsion to what you see as a confusion between 'the logical and psychological aspects of learning'. There may, perhaps, be a degree of confusion, but not, I think, a vicious or systematic confusion, in the document you criticise. In essence its argument rests on three major propositions, none of which seems to me to confuse logical with psychological issues : that an engagement with the major disciplines of thought may arise out of and be sustained by a multiplicity of experience other than those traditionally associated with the teaching of mathematics, science or the humanities as academic subjects in school; that the value of any body of experience in stimulating and sustaining involvement with the major disciplines of thought is in part dependent upon its capacity to arouse a pupil's interest and encourage his autonomy, though not of course dependent upon this alone; and that the consequence of recognising the intellectual value and potential of wider ranges of experience in an educational system which continually encourages autonomy will be to bring about, in the end, a certain reconstruction of knowledge and of culture (as sketched, for example, in the essay by Professor Hawkins to which I refer in my two articles for *Forum*).

To return to the more specific question of compulsion, you ask what happens if a teacher, with a commitment to teaching maths, never notices signs of involvement which he might turn to mathematical effort or if the student refuses to accept his efforts to turn them to the desired effect. My answer is that the teacher persists, introducing the student to mathematical activities and mathematical ideas, dwelling on mathematical significances, emphasising mathematical skills, asserting the value of mathematics as a discipline of thought and as a practical utility. One might almost go so far as to say that the teacher 'insists'. But insistence stops short of compulsion, for it is open to the student to reject the teacher's insistence without then being compelled to accept it. Here certainly is a major source of disagreement between us. You believe, I think, that accepting responsibility for our children entails compelling them to study what we believe to be educative for them. I deny this. I believe that compulsion (certainly within an upper school and quite possibly, in many ways, within a primary school) is an expedient which, though necessary on occasions and in particular circumstances, as a rule, or as a routine, is likely to be educationally damaging in the absence of the kind of motivation which renders it redundant.

There's a passage in R. S. Peters's *Ethics and Education* which I find useful in clarifying my own position on this point by way of contrast. Peters argues that 'we would not call a man "educated" who knew about science and who could go through the motions of scientific thought and experiment but who cared nothing for finding out the truth or who regarded science purely as a means to material advancement. [So much, incidentally, for the equation of 'cognitive' with 'instrumental' and 'expressive' with 'affective'.] But although to be "educated" he must eventually come to care about something like science in this way and make it his own, it does not follow that he must have been brought to care about it by educational processes which always enlisted his interest and encouraged his autonomous activity . . . The scientist may have been forced, while he was a boy, to do experiments in which he had not the slightest interest. But by being trained to do them repeatedly under rigorous supervision he may eventually have come to develop an interest in doing scientific experiments and gone out of his way to do them, irrespective of whether he was made to do them or not. Whether or not making boys do things in which they have no initial interest, without trying to harness them to their existing interests, is an effective technique, is an empirical question. The fact is that it has been practised in many educational institutions which have turned out educated and dedicated men. It might be argued that this has happened in spite of rather than because of the methods of instruction used. But this is an empirical question on which it would be rash to pronounce without a lot of evidence.'

As against Peters, I argue that unless educational processes DO commonly, though not necessarily invariably, enlist a student's interest and encourage his autonomous activity, then he IS unlikely to come to care about what he has been taught. Conversely I argue that where educated and dedicated men have emerged from institutions which failed to encourage their autonomous activity this is more likely than not to have *indeed* happened in spite of rather than because of the methods of instruction used. And I claim that this is a matter which can be determined, in some measure at any rate, without amassing such a weight of evidence as Peters seems to require. In short, I argue that the goal of autonomy, which

I accept, as does Peters himself, as a necessary condition of the educated man, is most likely to be achieved where the processes of education themselves continually encourage autonomous activity on the part of the pupil.

I have insisted on this point about compulsion because of its importance in my own thinking. But I should add that many of my Countesthorpe colleagues would probably feel less strongly committed to it than I do. And of course it would be wrong to suggest that, in our daily practice, there is no compulsion at Countesthorpe. There is, both inasmuch as attendance is compulsory and also in the everyday experience of students. None the less there is certainly a much larger measure of autonomy for students at Countesthorpe than is common in secondary schools, grammar, secondary modern or comprehensive, or indeed than would be in any way acceptable to a traditional concept of schooling, as you rightly surmise.

And so – at long last, I fear – to your two final and most fundamental criticisms. First you cite the characteristic reluctance of progressives to make discriminations and distinctions. I admit the charge in part. Of course there is always a problem to be faced in this respect by those who wish to revise entrenched discriminations or traditional distinctions. It is impossible to accept what are perceived to be corrupt or outworn distinctions, and yet it is hard to discriminate afresh without slipping back into the discarded terminology. This is partly what explains the 'blurred image' which progressive thought and practice at first, almost inevitably, conveys. Nevertheless, I would in no way wish to rely on this explanation as an excuse for imprecision or muddled thought. I accept, therefore, under your correction, that there is a distinction between 'academic concern' and 'pastoral care' as those terms are normally used. What I object to is the way in which this distinction is used to polarise learning into 'instrumental' and 'expressive' aspects, as for instance Bernbaum does, and to suggest that the two aspects, if not mutually exclusive, are at any rate wholly independent of each other. You write, of Highbury Grove, that 'while care was taken to foster good social relations in the school, the prime aim was academic, in line with Dr Boyson's belief that the purpose of schooling is learning. Dr Boyson in fact stressed the instrumental role of the school'. I would argue that academic concern and pastoral care are interdependent in a way which this passage seems to deny, inasmuch as an academic concern for most children's learning commonly entails pastoral care while pastoral care, in turn, within the context of schooling, entails an academic concern.

As for the distinction between 'affective' and 'cognitive', my feeling is that your own admission of the interconnections between the terms is enough for my purposes. I do not assert that there is no distinction but that the necessary discriminations are too subtle to be accommodated within a presumed polarisation of cultures, the one affective, the other cognitive.

For I agree with you that it is here, in our respective attitudes to the question of culture, that the heart of our disagreement lies. 'There are certain varieties of reality which are open to some and will for ever remain closed to others.' I reject both the implication of total discontinuity between the 'intellectual and cultural grasp' of 'the mass of the people', as Lawrence apparently calls them, and the cultural elite, and equally the presumption that such discontinuity as does exist is final and ineradicable. 'A fool sees not the same tree that a wise man sees.' Perhaps, but Blake, just ten proverbs later, goes on to say 'If the fool would persist in his folly he would become wise'. And are Blake's wisdom and folly really to be equated with 'cognitive' and 'affective' realms, the 'word of understanding' and the 'voice of dynamic sound'? That is hard to believe.

You enlist in your support 'the whole of human history' but history allows of more than one possible interpretation, even if one discounts the revolutionary consequences for literacy of the process of industrialisation. You say, for example, that St Thomas Aquinas and the mediaeval peasant did not worship the same God. I would set alongside that comment some remarks of the historian M. I. Finley which I have just come across in his recent book *The Use and Abuse of History*. He is discussing a statement to the effect that 'art of integrity is never likely to be popular . . . it is an art of cultivation, not immediately accessible, for not only its appreciation but its simple, casual enjoyment, depends upon a long apprenticeship'. But, argues Finley, 'tragedy in fifth century BC Athens was an act of integrity and it was popular; so has church music been in many places over long periods; even sermons, and I am thinking not of vulgar revivalist preachers but of the linguistically and intellectually complex sermons of Calvin and his followers, of John Donne, of other, perhaps lesser preachers to our own day. A long apprenticeship would no doubt have enhanced the understanding of these works but the mass audiences had no formal training, no apprenticeship in that sense. What they had was a sharing in the myths, beliefs and values which were the stuff of such works, to which they could therefore respond with concentrated attention and with simple, casual enjoyment. If, as is hardly disputable, our world knows nothing like Greek tragedy or Bach masses, in this respect, the possibility must surely be considered that what has changed is not some existential popular taste but the groundwork itself, that high culture is no longer moored to a broad, common language and common value system, that neither defeatism nor a rigid persistence with old pedagogical notions (which of course intensifies the defeatism) is the only possible response.'

From this somewhat different historical perspective I see nothing improbable or futile in the idea of a recovery of common language and common values through a reconstruction of knowledge achieved in part by the progressive reform of the structures and processes of education.

What set out to be a brief rejoinder seems to have turned into an inordinately discursive epistle. But it has been a pleasure and an excitement to mull over your letter and to respond to your criticisms. I hope that your history of educational thought will work out as you wish it to and I look forward to reading it, I hope before too long.

Best wishes,

Yours sincerely,
Michael Armstrong

18 August 1975

Dear Mr Armstrong,

Thank you for your letter of 30 April. I must apologise for the long delay in replying, but it did not seem to need an immediate reply, and I thought it, therefore, better to leave it to the vacation.

I think there are three points I want to take up with you; the questions of relevance, of compulsion, and of varieties of reality open to certain children. I may make a brief reference to the question of pastoral care.

Let me begin with the question of relevance. You quote Dixon's comment, with which you obviously agree. I don't totally understand the quotation, because I don't completely comprehend the force of the word 'metaphorically'. That apart, however, the suggestion of a widening circle from the immediate 'narrow circle of home and neighbourhood' seems to me to be misconceived and to be the root of much misconception in current educational practice. Perhaps my point here can be better made for me, in some respects, by Coleridge.

'For from my early reading of fairy tales and genii, etc., etc., my mind had been habituated *to the Vast*, and I never regarded *my senses* in any way as the criteria of my belief. I regulated all my creeds by my conceptions, not by my *sight*, even at that age. Should children be permitted to read romances, and relations of giants and magicians and genii? I know all that has been said against it; but I have formed my faith in the affirmative. I know no other way of giving the mind a love of the Great and the Whole. Those who have been led to the same truths step by step, through the constant testimony of their senses, seem to me to want a sense which I possess. They contemplate nothing but *parts*, and all *parts* are necessarily little. And the universe to them is but a mass of *little things*. It is true, that the mind may become credulous and prone to superstition by the former method; but are not the experimentalists credulous even to madness in believing any absurdity, rather than believe the grandest truths, if they have not the testimony of their own senses in their favour? I have known some who have been *rationally* educated, as it is styled. They were marked by a microscopic acuteness, but when they looked at great things, all became a blank and they saw nothing, and denied (very illogically) that anything could be seen, and uniformly put the negation of a power for the possession of a power, and called the want of imagination judgement and the never being moved to rapture philosophy!'

Now this may not be totally relevant to Dixon's remarks, but it does add something to the debate which I think is of great importance. Dixon's view of things leads to such manifestations as Leila Berg's *Nippers*, with their crude imitations of supposedly working-class language ('Cor, don't it pong!'). Children are often embarrassed by this sort of thing, and indeed there is no reason to suppose that they want certain manifestations of their own existence thrust down their throats at school. Some years ago Musgrove did an investigation which indicated that children were far more interested in and wrapped up in history which was remote in time and place rather than in the history on their own doorstep. Indeed there might be good reason for starting with the exotic and moving towards the mundane, which seems to be the opposite process of what Dixon is recommending. (Often, indeed, the exotic, e.g. Greek myths, is more 'relevant' than the ephemera of their own doorsteps.) Therefore, relevance is a concept which needs to be interpreted with much care. Clearly one does not want something which is totally incomprehensible to the child, but one does want him to aspire after the as yet unknown, which, with due regard to the value of the experience, is the fundamental purpose of education.

Then I come on to the question of compulsion. Here I find that you tend to hedge a little, as all progressives tend to hedge. Thus you say 'unless educational processes DO commonly, though not necessarily invariably, enlist a student's interest and encourage his autonomous activity then he IS unlikely to come to care about what he has been taught'. Well, how common is 'commonly', how invariant is 'invariably'. It reminds me a little of Dewey's point about not imposing anything on children, but the teacher being there 'as a member of the community to select the influences which shall affect the child and to assist him in properly responding to these influences'; I am always tempted to ask what happens to those who don't properly respond? But these subtleties apart, I am sure there is here a fundamental division between us. Clearly any skilful teacher will have regard to the potential, intellectual and emotional, of his charges, and clearly he will seek to motivate his students. But we must face up to the fact that, normally, at some stage at least, some imposition will be necessary. First, even interests flag, and where young children are concerned flag very quickly. Secondly, a child cannot know what he is interested in until he has been made to sample at least an offering. I recall, in this connection, a remark made by Jacqueline du Pré, the famous cellist. In a radio interview she spoke of how grateful she was to her mother who *made* her practise as a child. Gifted as she was, she did not wish to undertake the labour concerned, but her mother insisted, with the result that she became world famous as a practitioner, as you are well aware. Again I recall a student in our own department when this issue was under discussion. He said he had always hated economics, but, forced to undertake it for an examination for some qualification in transport, he had gradually acquired a taste. Having got the opportunity to come to the university after the war, he took economics as an honours degree. He would have nothing of your libertarian philosophy. Well, only two instances, but real instances. Clearly I would not persist in a child's musical education, if, after a time, I became convinced that he had neither interest nor aptitude, but I would certainly insist on the initial experiment. So you find me agreeing with Peters rather than with you. Incidentally, I think the conception of 'autonomy' needs careful philosophical analysis. All too often it comes to mean accepting the values of the peer group rather than those of the teacher's culture.

Thirdly, the question as to the varieties of reality open to some people. I think I have mentioned that my wife teaches remedial reading. Some of the children she is concerned with have considerable potential, because they are victims of emotional disturbance rather than lacking in intellect. But there are some who are *just dull*. In any case, for certain sorts of achievement one needs more than simply intellect – one also needs, perhaps, a stable background. Therefore, it seems to me, we must be willing to make discriminations, and offer to children what, on either intellectual or emotional grounds, or both, they can cope with. Indeed, part of the function of the primary school is diagnostic. It is all very well talking about the sermons of Calvin and Donne, or, for that matter, the plays of Shakespeare; but Shakespeare knew that his plays were understood at different levels by different sections of the society which attended them. And in characters like Dogberry, he satirises those who get little beyond the sound and complexity of words without genuine understanding. People in those days had more respect for learning and language, but it does not mean, necessarily, that they had all equally full comprehension. This I believe profoundly to be the human condition, i.e. a great diversity of levels of cognitive competence, and I think this must be accepted as a prime datum of the educational situation. (Some recent work in science education would seem to bear out what I am saying – and do you know Hallam's work on history?)

Finally, with regard to the question of pastoral care, Pastoral care, I feel, must be directed towards the implementation of the ends and aims of school learning. The teacher is not a social worker.

Well, it has been an interesting debate, and I suppose has revealed fairly fundamental divisions of opinion which now exercise the educational world. But I believe research is beginning to bear out my views, and indeed one could almost say that the new 'in' word is 'structure'! I suppose, finally, it is arguable that one of the purposes of education is a socio-cultural one, to keep the culture going, and the excessive egocentricity of romantic progressivism, in the last resort, does ill service to the public welfare.

Yours sincerely,
G. H. Bantock
Professor of Education

1 October 1975

Dear Professor Bantock,

Your letter was waiting for me on my return from holiday at the end of August. In one way and another it's been on my mind ever since and now, at the risk of repetitiveness, I'd like to offer some kind of response to each of its three arguments. I hope that in doing so I may be able to add something to the debate between us and between 'traditionalism' and 'progressivism' in general.

First, then, the argument about relevance. I'm not certain that we disagree that much. At any rate I find myself in strong sympathy with the substance of your magnificent quotation from Coleridge. And yet I see no reason to suppose that Coleridge's plea for romance and fairy tale contradicts John Dixon's insistence that teaching should begin with whatever experiences children can identify as important and valuable to themselves, experiences which will necessarily reflect, on many occasions and in many ways, what Dixon calls 'the narrow circle of home and neighbourhood'. For this is the world in which children have grown up, in which they have already begun to form their most powerful insights into the nature of men and of things. It may be a narrow world but that does not mean that it is insignificant, lacking in depth or universality. To identify the circle of home and neighbourhood with Coleridge's 'mass of little things', with a lack of 'power', 'imagination' or 'rapture', is to take every bit as superficial a view of the child's world as that which is implied by the very worst of the *Nippers* readers which you criticise.

But that being said, I accept that a concern for relevance is set to be identified with what you call the 'ephemera of our own doorsteps'. I acknowledge the relevance of the exotic. Indeed I think this is what Dixon himself had in mind in referring to the way in which teaching materials may reflect a child's concerns metaphorically as well as directly. Equally, I accept that the purpose of education is 'to aspire after the as yet unknown', a point on which, by the way, Dixon is no less explicit than yourself. But the achievement of such aspirations depends, I believe, on a continual interplay between the as yet unknown and the already familiar, between the insights and intuitions explored in the beginning within the narrow circle of home and neighbourhood and these new worlds of knowledge which children will come to explore within the context of a rich and open-textured environment at school. It is when each of these orders of experience resonates with the power of the other that knowledge comes alive.

You imply that, as far as schooling is concerned, it is enough that the matter presented to children by teachers should not be 'totally incomprehensible' to them. That is quite inadequate. Children need to do more than understand the bare sense of whatever it is they are being asked to study. It is also necessary for them to appreciate its significance in the light of their own present experience and understanding, to feel that it is worthy of their concern and commitment. This is why you are right to insist on the relevance of romance. For the world of romance is embedded within the most vital and universal experiences of childhood. The study of myths, of distant times and places, of strange and exotic forms of life, has therefore a special power to engage the commitment of children by reflecting some of their most deeply felt experiences while simultaneously leading them on to the exploration of new worlds of understanding. This I take to be part of Coleridge's meaning as it also is one part of Dixon's meaning. I find its finest expression in an article by Tolstoy about his school for peasant children on his estate. Part of this article is reprinted in Aylmer Maude's translation of Tolstoy's essays on art (*What is Art?*, World Classics, 1930) but as far as I know its educational significance has rarely been noticed. Yet I know of no other piece of writing which demonstrates so well how Coleridge's 'power', 'imagination' and 'rapture', 'a love of the Great and the whole', flourish within the context of a 'free', or 'progressive', or 'child-centred', education, an education centred on the imaginative power of the child's own experience and on the teacher's ability to help him extend it into the most complex forms of knowledge. I am sending with this letter a copy of a new translation of this passage by my friend Alan Pinch. It seems to me to be of great importance to the issues we are debating.

Next, the question of compulsion. Whenever, as in your letter, I am told of some 'fact' which I 'must face up to' I suspect that I am being urged to accept without question someone else's unquestioned assumption. And so it is that here I want to cast doubt on each one of your categorical assertions about compulsion.

1. It is not true that young children's interests flag very quickly. Often, indeed, as every parent is ruefully forced to recognise, their interests are obsessively, even absurdly, persistent. I am tempted to argue that the interests which seem, to parents or teachers, to flag very quickly are those which they want to impose while the interests which maddingly persist are those which they want to eradicate. But that would be tendentious. At any rate we often misunderstand the force and direction of children's interests in our anxiety to adapt them to our own convenience and taste, or to our own purposes.

Yet 'even interests flag'. Of course. But the waning of interest does not in itself justify imposition, as you seem to assume. It is a cardinal, if common, mistake in teaching to force a child to pursue a line of inquiry the moment he looses interest in it. Nothing does more to diminish the value of inquiry in the eyes of children. Of course the best teachers, whatever their ideology, rarely if ever act in this way. Instead, they look for reasons why their pupils are losing interest, they hold back for a while, they encourage persistence in times of difficulty or boredom, they explore fresh ways of kindling enthusiasm and engaging commitment, they wait, they begin on something new. In the end imposition usually turns out to be as unnecessary as it is undesirable. If you ask why I should be so wary of imposition, why go to such lengths to avoid it, why consider it so damaging, I would answer that to substitute an external, imposed authority for an intrinsic, personal commitment is to weaken the very aspirations which, as you agree, it is the ultimate purpose of education to foster – 'giving the mind a love of the Great and the Whole' as Coleridge puts it. Although Coleridge was ambiguous in his attitude towards the educational practice of his day he never doubted the centrality of a sense of personal commitment in any education which was to be worthy of the name. So he writes of Plato's theory of education that 'the education of the intellect, by awakening the principle and method of self development, was his proposed object, not any specific information that can be conveyed into it from without. Not to assist in storing the passive mind with the various sort of knowledge most in request, as if the human soul were a mere repository . . . but to place it in such relations of circumstance as should gradually excite the germinal power that craves no knowledge but what it can take up into itself, what it can appropriate and re-produce in fruits of its own. To shape, to dye, to paint over, and to mechanize the mind, he resigned as their proper trade to the sophists.'

2. It is not true that 'a child cannot know what he is interested in until HE HAS BEEN MADE TO sample at least an offering'. Starting to learn something does not entail having to learn it. To suppose that it does is to take an implausibly dim view of the curiosity of children and of the resourcefulness of teachers. In a thriving school or home the context in which 'initial experiments' in learning take place is likely to be one in which the children's expectations are already aroused, and their interest already engaged. Here, for example, is how Tolstoy describes the introduction of singing lessons into his school. It is not the only way to begin and the initiative might just as well, in different circumstances, have come from the teacher rather than the pupils. But it does, I think, draw attention to the kind of bond between present experience and future possibility which is as important in beginning to learn something as it is in sustaining the learning.

'Last summer we were coming back from bathing. We were all feeling very gay. A peasant boy, a thick set boy with wide cheek bones, covered all over in freckles, with crooked legs turned inwards, having all the mannerisms of an adult peasant of the steppes, but an intelligent, strong and gifted nature, ran forward and took a seat in a cart which was driving in front of us. He took the reins, pushed his hat askew, spat to one side and burst out in some long-drawn-out peasant song – and how he sang – feelingly, with rests and sudden bursts of song. The lads burst out laughing. "Look at Syomka, look at Syomka, doesn't he play it fine?" Syomka was completely serious. "Here you, don't interrupt the song" he said during an interval in a special, deliberately husky voice, and gravely continued his singing. Two of the most musical boys took seats on the cart, began to seek harmonies and sang them. One was harmonising now in an eighth, now in a sixth, the other in a third, and it turned out excellently. Then other boys came up and began to sing "As under such an apple tree". They started shouting and the result was noisy but no good. The singing began with that evening.'

My argument is that 'experiments' in learning which are not, in some such way as this, rooted in children's experience will rarely engage the quality of commitment essential to their success. A fine contemporary account of how such experiments begin can be found in a book called *The Logic of Action*, by Frances Hawkins, in which she describes a period of observation and participation in a kindergarten for deaf children. I would recommend her book to anyone who still believes that to encourage children to take a large part in the design of their own learning is to leave them to get on as they please. I have already mentioned my own attempt to describe the same process of starting an inquiry in a recent article in *Forum* on the work of a 16-year-old student I used to teach.

3. I find your two instances of the value of compulsion unilluminating. I would need to know so much more about the context in which Jacqueline du Pré's mother 'made' her practice. I strongly suspect that Jacqueline du Pré enjoyed playing, loved music, got on well at it and was strongly committed to it. No doubt her mother still had to insist on the importance of her practising, and even, in some senses on some occasions, make her practise, but always against a background of direct personal concern for music on her daughter's part. And that seems to me to be the critical factor. Your second example, admittedly, is *prima facie* evidence on the other side and there can be no doubt that some children do sometimes come to enjoy what first they have been forced to study against their will. But I believe that this is often despite rather than because of being forced and that there is probably an inverse ratio between the frequency of compulsion and the frequency of enjoyment.

I have already, of course, admitted in a previous letter that compulsion may sometimes be reasonable and even essential and I cannot take seriously your suggestion that to admit this much is to 'hedge'. My point is quite simple that compulsion should be the exception rather than the rule and that when it becomes the rule then it tends to stifle the growth of that personal commitment to knowledge which is our common goal. Frances Hawkins puts it well, I think, in a note about one of her 4-year-old kindergarten pupils. 'For Phillip the printed word is not yet much needed or of much use. It will be if well integrated with his primary concerns: exploring the physical world, admiring its phenomena, and insatiably observing and experimenting. If reading and writing are pushed at him before he sees how they fit his needs, his defences of boredom and daydreaming will be called up against what is still irrelevant for him, and his learning slowed. Just as we have seen him teach himself with open-ended materials, so he will, if not forced, make the printed word his own. Boys like Phillip succeed under their own banners and fail only when squeezed into a rigid time-scale or narrow method during early and vulnerable times in their lives. Who does not understand these basic truths? Only those who, by not providing a rich environment – with open-ended "raw" materials – rule out the setting in which the Phillips exemplify how learning proceeds for them, how much they can teach and how well pace themselves.'

Much the same point crops up in an essay of Jerome Bruner's which discusses the 'will to learn' from a more specifically psychological viewpoint. I find it interesting to set the one alongside the other. 'The will to learn', Bruner suggests, 'is an intrinsic motive, one that finds both its source and its reward in its own exercise. The will to learn becomes a "problem" only under specialised circumstances like those of a school, where a curriculum is set, students confined, and a path fixed. The problem exists not so much in learning itself, but in the fact that what the school imposes often fails to enlist the natural energies that sustain spontaneous learning – curiosity, a desire for competence, aspiration to emulate a model, and a deep-sensed commitment to the web of social reciprocity . . . You will have noted by now a considerable de-emphasis of "extrinsic" rewards and punishments as factors in school learning. I am not unmindful of the notion of reinforcement. It is doubtful only that "satisfying states of affairs" are reliably to be found outside learning itself – in kind or harsh words from the teacher, in grades and gold stars, in the absurdly abstract assurance to the high school student that his lifetime earnings will be better by 80 per cent if he graduates. External reinforcement may indeed get a particular act going and may even lead to its repetition, but it does not nourish, reliably, the long course of learning by which man slowly builds in his own way a serviceable model of what the world is and what it can be.'

I agree.

Lastly the question of varieties of reality. I am not altogether clear what your phrase 'a great diversity of levels of cognitive competence' is intended to mean. You seem to believe in a hierarchy of realities, discrete cultural worlds more or less mutually exclusive. You seem to imply that such a hierarchy is not simply the contingent reflection of particular social structures in particular societies but rather as inevitable aspect of the human condition.

As I suggested in my last letter, I see no reason to accept this interpretation of history, culture and individual psychology, for all its ancient pedigree and perennial appeal. In so far as it is in principle possible to weigh the 'evidence' in support of a particular image of man, my own experience, study and reflection suggest, inevitably perhaps, a somewhat different balance from that which appeals to you. Among the more recent researches I have looked at, I have found especially interesting the work of those anthropologists, linguists, psychologists and others who have been studying the cultural context of language, thought and learning. Their studies make it easier to recognise how, as Michael Cole and his fellow psychologists put it at the end of their book *The Cultural Context of Learning and Thinking*, 'cultural differences in cognition reside more in the situations to which particular cognitive processes are applied than in the existence of a process in one cultural group and its absence in another'. Part of this body of research derives from the work of the linguist Benjamin Lee Whorf whose viewpoint is worth citing, perhaps, in contrast to your own hierarchical conception. 'The scientific understanding of very diverse language', according to Whorf, 'is a lesson in brotherhood which is brotherhood in the universal human principle . . . It causes to transcend the boundaries of local cultures, nationalities, physical pecularities dubbed "race", and to find that in their linguistic systems, though these systems differ widely, yet in the order, harmony, and beauty of the systems, and in their respective subtleties and penetrating analysis of reality, all men are equal.'

I would want to distinguish, as I think you do not, between hierarchy and diversity. 'Progressive' education rests on a presumption that children, not just a privileged few but almost all of them, are capable of an imaginative and rational understanding of reality, of grasping the fundamental truths of science, humanities, mathematics, the arts. But at the same time 'progressive' education assumes that there are innumerable ways that lead towards this common understanding, reflecting the extraordinary wealth and variety of intellect and imagination to be found among children, or for that matter among adults. To recognise the richness of this diversity is to commit oneself not merely to a wider dissemination of knowledge but to a reconstruction of many of its forms and contents. By contrast, as I see it, 'traditional' education is incapable of appreciating, let alone fostering, the diversity of intellect of which you write because it is trapped by its obsession with establishing a narrow intellectual hierarchy that obscures both the common potential and the astonishing diversity of children. Hence, I think, your readiness to describe some of your wife's pupils as 'just dull'. I would not care to be a pupil whose teacher considered him 'dull'. And indeed I have never yet come across a child I could justly describe in this way. It seems to me that dullness we think to detect in children is really no more than a symptom of our own frustration at being unable to engage their interest, excite their imagination, or foster their intellect. More than anything, it reflects the constricting narrowness of our received ideas about intellectual understanding and intellectual growth.

For the present we must agree to differ but the argument will continue. During the past five years of teaching at Countesthorpe I have certainly come to understand more clearly how hard it is to pursue the 'progressive' goal. But I have also begun to catch sight of the richness of its promise.

Yours sincerely,
Michael Armstrong

PART VIII

WHAT IT MEANS TO OTHERS

21

What It Means to Others

HARRY RÉE

HARRY RÉE has had a distinguished career. As an undergraduate at Cambridge in the thirties he met Henry Morris, who pioneered the Cambridgeshire Village Colleges. In 1973 Longman published Harry Rée's book on Morris, Educator Extraordinary.

In 1951 Rée became headmaster of Watford Grammar School and in 1962 he went to York as the university's first professor of education. On retiring from that chair in 1974, he returned to the fray by resuming modern languages teaching on the staff of an inner London comprehensive school. He also continues to write, broadcast and organise action where he sees the need for it.

Harry Rée has visited Countesthorpe regularly and is now convinced that, far from being the isolated one-off venture that some observers have labelled it, the experience has considerable significance for others today.

We are grateful to him for contributing this article to the book.

Educational evolution proceeds by jumps. Each new development, or 'sport', appears on the scene unexpectedly and survives only if climate and environment are favourable. It dies off, becomes extinct, if it isn't fit to survive. In the 1830s Thomas Arnold re-shaped Rugby and, because at that period the climate was favourable, his new model public school flourished and reproduced itself for about a hundred years. Another educational 'sport' appeared in the early years of the nineteenth century, the monitorial system, independently put into practice by Lancaster and Bell. The system was ideally designed for the teaching of large numbers of poor children by small numbers of low-paid teachers – this suited the philosophy and economic climate of the time – so for many years it flourished.

McMullen and Watts (unlike Lancaster and Bell) worked in tandem; they too may well be another such influential pair, while the new model, at Countesthorpe, may come to be seen as the first of a series, a species even, of schools which promote a system of education, cunningly adjusted and attuned to the mood and climate of the last decades of this century. So although already Countesthorpe has been an important influence upon the pupils of a suburban village in Leicestershire, this is nothing compared with what Countesthorpe has already done, is now doing and may continue increasingly to do, to influence the development of schools and of education not only in this country in this century, but abroad as well.

It's also true to say that given a change of climate, given massive and prolonged discouragement instead of informed support, Countesthorpe could soon fade, forgotten as the dream it began as. Then it would merely occupy a short paragraph in twenty-first-century histories of education in England. This would be tragic because it would mean that the world outside the school – and I don't just mean the surroundings of Countesthorpe or of Leicester but the world we are a part of – had pessimistically looked back and turned to unfertile salt. It would mean that the high hopes for life, for a more abundant life for everyone, had been replaced in England with low expectations for survival. Teachers however have to be optimists, so I write hopefully. Already Countesthorpe has attracted more attention (often unhelpful) than any maintained school ever before. It ranks with 'That dreadful school' (Summerhill) or 'Liberty Hall' (Dartington) as an arouser of spleen in some and delight in others. The fact that it is a maintained school, and not one of the family of privileged progressives, is significant, because this reveals a fund of self-confidence, always a necessary attribute of successful innovators, which until now has been found only among the independents. The state school has, as it were, come of age.

All innovation is painful, and the new thoughts and practice engendered at Countesthorpe have not only encountered noisy as well as silent opposition, they have met with their fair share of the 'dynamic conservatism' described by David Schon in his recent Reith Lectures as being the more sophisticated reaction of an established system to the threat of change. This is, still according to Schon, often accompanied by 'irrelevant action', taking the form of pseudo-innovation as a means of repelling would-be reformers. Such practices as mixed-ability teaching in a grammar school or the admission of a ration of girls to a boys' public school are obvious examples of 'irrelevant action'. But history is on the side of radical innovation; for an institution to stand still is a recipe for being overtaken, and the ideas which move Countesthorpe forward (oppur si muove!) move it in step with other innovating institutions. So it is enlightened foresight, as well perhaps as fame, that is the spur for Countesthorpe, and for those schools which are moving with it.

Enlightened foresight certainly moved McMullen, who himself underwent a change of philosophy in mid-career. The comprehensive school of which he was head before Countesthorpe was an early model and owed much to the theories of the fifties, and perhaps to McMullen's own public school experience. Before being appointed to Countesthorpe he did much thinking, and became aware that since the world was changing fast the schools must change too. New attitudes to authority, new inventions and industrial systems, new developments both in primary and in post-school education, all these threatened the traditional school. He saw that a defensive stance would be a recipe for defeat and eventual irrelevance. Unlike many who saw salvation merely in the establishment of comprehensive education, or in ROSLA, or in the introduction of new courses, or new methods of teaching, McMullen recognised that, while all these things were desirable and necessary, if they were to be successful they should not be planted in the traditional school if they were going to constitute more than 'irrelevant action'. The original Newsom child, with his : 'It might be made of marble, sir, but it's still a bloody school', was saying the same things as McMullen; he had spotted what McMullen spotted and decided to eliminate, the rotten apple at the bottom of the barrel, and that rotten apple was destructive conflict leading to unnecessary repression.

Basic to McMullen's thinking has been the conviction that in education, conflict, especially covert conflict, is seldom productive and often inhibiting. Within the schools he saw two areas where conflict was growing, and growing more pernicious : between teachers and taught, and between teachers and heads. There were of course other areas, in particular where the school and representatives of the world outside failed to agree; here too conflict was growing and a solution was needed.

In the past such conflicts were contained or even resolved, either because many assumptions were shared across the divide, or because the staff imposed their will ultimately by physical fear. In the sixties it became clear that we could no longer rely on shared assumptions; in John Watts's words, a shared set of values 'is something we have not got'; at the same time it was increasingly recognised that physical fear was no longer either acceptable or efficient as a means of containing conflict or of inducing learning.

No longer supported by shared values, nor effectively shored up by physical threats, the school became increasingly vulnerable, and we passed through the valley of the shadow, when the very survival of the school was debated. To keep it in being, increasing reliance was placed on the scaffolding provided by the traditional hierarchy, and yet it was this, seen by many as the one essential support, which fed the fires of destructive conflict. Courageously McMullen decided to remove that scaffolding, to dismantle the hierarchy. At Countesthorpe he aimed to do himself, as headmaster, out of a job, to make himself redundant, and in place of the old supports an agreed system of power-sharing would be established. This involved a risk. There was a vacuum period when Countesthorpe seemed unable to find any alternative means of support, while the head and the staff, the students and the governors energetically but vainly sought ways of organising the sharing of power so that a cohesive institution would emerge, which would be able energetically to pursue agreed aims. Under Watts ways were found; he himself remains at the head, and will continue to do so, but as the previous chapters show, if Countesthorpe isn't quite out of the wood, it is out of the dark forest.

The lesson now available for others is simple; it's a lesson about orders of priority. The first objective, in strategic terms, is power-sharing across the board. The first target therefore to be tackled is the power structure of the school; but this needs to be done in no mindless or violent way.

The operation needs time, thought and an agreed strategy. Different institutions will go about the task in different ways, each one seeing particular areas where destructive and now removable conflict have in the past seemed a part of life. For instance in the area of teaching and learning, steps might be taken towards a negotiated curriculum for each child. Such treaties open the door to autonomy, to new and productive relationships, and above all to a commitment by the pupils to their own individual progress but at the same time, perhaps unwittingly at first, to a commitment to the common and wider aims of the school. In the area of decision-making hesitant steps forward may be attempted through genuine all-through consultation on the curriculum, on school organisation, on the distribution of resources between clamouring claimants, and on the sharing of responsibility with all the staff concerned, for promotions and appointments. But all such attempts at reform, even if they go some way, are tinkling cymbals, unless the main target is kept constantly in view.

For to attempt to introduce reforms within the traditional framework of the school, having allowed the main target to be forgotten, is to tempt failure; for if the intermediate reforms fall short of expectations, perhaps don't even work, then the pressure for genuine reform, which is to be achieved only through power-sharing, will be weakened, discredited and probably deflated.

The question must now be put. If there is a head, or a staff, or a governing body that wants to implement the ideas represented by Countesthorpe, what steps need to be taken? Many would answer: none. Many would contend that Countesthorpe started with such massive advantages that, even if the will to imitate were there, the means for others to do so are not. Countesthorpe had its 'tailored' architecture, its specially selected staff, and for once the opportunity was there to order new and appropriate resources and materials. What other school is not hampered by its buildings designed for a previous era, or for a different philosophy, by a disunited staff, and by real or impending 'cuts'? And so the crocodiles tearfully say 'no'. But while such a response is to be expected from many, it should be remembered that it is the obvious response of those who in fact don't want to change.

Others, happily, are less negative; they are prepared to accept as a fact of life that they are burdened with disadvantages Countesthorpe had not got; it is not possible therefore for them to implement, as Countesthorpe tried to do, a whole package of reforms at one time. But this, as Watts sees it, can be an advantage; while a further benefit which an established school has over the embryo Countesthorpe is the existence of actual rather than prospective parents and of a known community with whom plans and possibilities can be fully discussed until they are understood, and accepted. But there are, of course, pitfalls. The danger of indulging in 'irrelevant action' isn't confined to those who don't want effective action. A school might decide that, as a start, from one term to another, staff as well as children should be called by their first names. Such action would lead more likely to sniggers by children and disapproval by parents than to a reduction in conflict between staff and pupils. Not that this implies that the question of how children address children is not important; it's as important as the question of how staff address children, and at some time, if the hierarchy is to be flattened, it must be tackled, but hardly as a first priority.

Nor does this caveat imply that a school might not make certain moves to reduce conflict by other means before introducing a fully-fledged moot where the vote of the head counts for as much as the vote of anyone else. In fact the moot, and even more important the rotating standing committee, might be established in the first instance as forums for discussion, with the only decisions taken being intermediate decisions about desirable policy and these would need a further vote at a later date for implementation. This would give time for discussions not only with existing and prospective parents but also with other bodies outside the school who might not have had a chance to take part in the original discussions.

There can be no doubt that there are an increasing number of teachers who accept McMullen's analysis of the situation in schools and its relation to changing conditions outside. They would agree that the first step is to reduce destructive conflict in the school through flattening the hierarchy. But we're in a strange, almost a Catch 22 situation, when the one individual who needs to be convinced of the necessity for flattening the hierarchy is the one who, it might seem, will be the first to be flattened; namely the head. And yet there is a way round; Watts makes it clear in Chapter 15 that he has used the traditional power he receives as a head to promote the sharing of power as planned by his predecessor. In so doing he has engaged in an exercise in power-shedding. But by a strange process, not governed by the laws of physics, in shedding his load he has increased his load. Perhaps it would be more true to say that in shedding his power he has increased his influence – and while it is accepted that he has great influence within the school, both he and the school have had, and will continue to have, great influence beyond the school.

Already a number of heads in different parts of the country have been appointed who are looking with undisguised interest in the direction of Countesthorpe. Some of them are already moving along the road, possibly moving their staff and governors with them towards genuine power-sharing, towards a genuine elimination of their own power, in return, of course, for an increase in their influence. As this movement grows, Countesthorpe will cease to have the unique importance and magnetic attraction for visitors which it has at the moment; doubtless no one will be more pleased about this relief than the head, the staff, the pupils and the governors of the College. But they can also be proud.

22

Countesthorpe in an International Context

ROBERT NORRIS

ROBERT NORRIS has travelled widely in business, teaching, school administration and service with the Ford Foundation. In 1973 he became an IMTEC fellow with Per Dalin, based in Oslo. He is currently working on a PhD in organisation behaviour at Yale University.

In 1973 he was chosen by IMTEC (International Management Training for Educational Change) to visit Countesthorpe and prepare up-to-date material for detailed case study. In the course of his visit he spent time in the College and interviewed a range of people locally and nationally, including Stewart Mason and the editor of the Leicester Mercury. *Since then he has received papers and bulletins from England relating to Countesthorpe and with Per Dalin (who has also visited Countesthorpe) organised two international seminars in Oslo where the innovation at Countesthorpe was subject to analysis and scrutiny. He is therefore ideally placed to comment on the significance that Countesthorpe has had for Europe and North America, and we are grateful to him and Per Dalin for the preparation of the following paper.*

INTRODUCTION

The purpose of this chapter is twofold: (a) to place the Countesthorpe experience in an international context of change in secondary education and (b) to give some background on the international interest in Countesthorpe. I will attempt to do this by addressing four questions:

1 Why has Countesthorpe been the focus of so much interest internationally?
2 What does Countesthorpe seem to have in common with developments in secondary education in other countries?
3 What makes Countesthorpe unique among these?
4 How can studies of Countesthorpe be used productively in the future?

Before beginning, let me partially clarify my perspective and biases. An American citizen with experience as a teacher and school administrator in the States, I joined the staff of IMTEC* in January 1973 and became immediately involved in updating the original OECD/CERI† case study on Countesthorpe which was done in 1971 about six months after the school opened. My goal, unlike that of the original case writer, was to make a learning package out of the data on the school for use in IMTEC training activities. I employed only a general interview guide and did not follow up on the questionnaire information that served as a basis for the first study. The product of my one week at the school (during which there was a major fire in the central core of the building) included many pounds of written material, interview and observation notes and several hundred questions about the change process which participants in the forthcoming IMTEC seminar could work on. Subsequent to that seminar, which was held in June 1973, I have been responsible for continuous IMTEC monitoring of Countesthorpe developments.

I mention the above so the reader will not presume that what follows is based on empirical data. It is opinion which has grown out of the Countesthorpe study and contact with educational leaders from fifteen countries, opinion tempered by reading and hundreds of hours with IMTEC colleagues discussing the nature of the change process. The responsibility for the ideas expressed in this chapter are completely mine, however.

WHY HAS COUNTESTHORPE BEEN THE FOCUS OF SO MUCH INTEREST INTERNATIONALLY?

There is no more generally (and hotly) debated issue in secondary education in Europe today than the issue of *comprehensive* schools, a term which, in my opinion, means much more than merely combining academic programmes with more practical or vocationally oriented education. It seems, according to political rhetoric, to imply major social restructuring. Even in Sweden, probably Europe's most centralised school system and one which has managed to achieve 100 per cent implementation of comprehensive secondary education after ten years of controlled experimentation and expansion, the issue continues as a major one between the political right and left. In Germany the issue has been so hot politically that implementation of comprehensive education correlates almost perfectly with the party in power in the various states. Though the issue has been a major plank in party platforms in Germany since the early sixties, there

* International Management Training for Educational Change, a decentralised project of the OECD's Centre for Educational Research and Innovation, designed to provide training and support for school innovators from member countries.

† Organisation for Economic Co-operation and Development/Centre for Educational Research and Innovation.

is very low overall acceptance of the idea. It is pure conjecture, but I suspect, on a spectrum of 'comprehensiveness' from Sweden to Germany, England would lie closer to Germany, its decentralised system showing a spotty development of comprehensives based on the politics of various regions (LEAs) and the nature of particular key leaders (e.g. Stuart Mason).

Despite the political upheaval surrounding comprehensives, there is a general movement in Europe and North America towards making educational opportunity more equal. Thus, there is social momentum towards forms of secondary education that are structured more equitably than the traditional selective systems that all too often perpetuate class distinctions and general social inequality. This social momentum translates directly through political processes to pressure on educators to innovate, to find new school forms that not only follow societal changes, but that address, in new ways, the changing needs of the 14- to 18-year-old.

From the Malmø region in Sweden, to Berlin, to the Experimental Schools Program in the USA, these pressures produced new leaders, new forms for brick and mortar, new organisational structures and new programmes. At national levels the needs of teenage students were translated into new policy terms like 'career education', 'education for cultural pluralism' and the creation of 'alternates within the system'. Regions or LEAs began developing experimental supports for innovations while balancing political tightropes, attempting to address pressures from the right and left, pressures from above at the national level and from below at the local school, parent and student level. But it was at the local school level that significant innovations have been taking form, sometimes in spite of the political confusion and shaky support from above.

It is in the context of all the above that Countesthorpe has been found to be so interesting. Stuart Mason's two-tier comprehensive system (which, he told me, came to him one morning while shaving) seemed to address the equality issue in a structural way not dissimilar to the American junior high–senior high system. But more emerged from that productive shave than a new form for making schools in Leicestershire comprehensive; the new schools were going to contain entirely new ways of meeting the needs of 11–18-year-olds, ways that cannot be prescribed by central office officials but must be developed at the school level by the headmaster and the staff working closely and informally with students and their parents.

No person could fit the local initiative model in Mason's mind better than Tim McMullen who, with his exceptionally able staff, moved into one of England's most modern comprehensives in 1970 and began to build Countesthorpe, the 'school of the future', a school with unusual sense for the needs of young people and a highly committed staff, a school where everyone would be learners and where decisions would be made by consensus in a 'moot'.

McMullen and Mason both had extensive international contacts. Mason was particularly known for elementary innovations in Leicestershire and McMullen had distinguished himself in the Nuffield Foundation and his previous experience as a headmaster. I don't honestly know how the decision was made to commission the 1971 CERI study of Countesthorpe but I don't recall great reluctance on the part of McMullen or his staff to become internationally visible, even if the school was only six months old. The resultant case study was dramatic and controversial and produced considerable concern among the staff members that the predictions made in the study were not, indeed, valid. Thus, in 1973, though McMullen had left, the staff and new headmaster, John Watts, were willing to be re-studied, if for no other reason than to set the record straight in the forth-coming IMTEC seminar. This seminar was followed by another in which Countesthorpe, now a very well documented 'living' case study, was a major training element. I suppose that through IMTEC activities to date Countesthorpe has been studied by no less than 150 international educa-tors. IMTEC network members frequently contact the school when in Eng-land and IMTEC keeps an up-to-date file on developments for use in future training.

In addition to IMTEC-related exposure, I know that French and Italian TV teams have visited the school to make documentaries. I don't know where they got the idea but it could have been a spin-off of OECD contacts. The school has boarding facilities and often has foreign students in resi-dence. I believe it has a 'sister' school in France to which Countesthorpe students can travel. Lastly, the school has received a great deal of inter-national attention through the extensive reports on its development in *The Times Educational Supplement*.

WHAT DOES COUNTESTHORPE SEEM TO HAVE IN COMMON WITH DEVELOP-MENTS IN SECONDARY EDUCATION IN OTHER COUNTRIES?

Though I have not made comparative studies of similar type innovations, my experience tells me that the Countesthorpe developments are similar to those in other countries in at least five areas: (a) its comprehensive design; (b) the political forces surrounding its development; (c) the idea of creating an 'alternative' within the system; (d) some of its organisational features; and (e) some of its curricular developments. It is necessary to look briefly at these features before turning to look at what makes the school unique from an international perspective.

First it is a *comprehensive* school, built under the Leicestershire two-tier model. Though it opened with students from 11 to 14 years of age, it was designed for the 14 to 18 range and is now functioning at that level. At this level of operation it is similar to a four-year American high school or the large comprehensives of Scandinavia. Students in the Countesthorpe attendance zone are free to attend without any form of 11-plus or other entrance requirements. The programme offered allows students to pursue various career options from O level and A level work to vocational and non-university-oriented programmes. As a true comprehensive, it has students from all social and economic backgrounds engaging in widely distributed course options.

It has become almost a cliche of the students of educational change to say that the more an innovation deviates from accepted practice, the more tension it will experience *vis-à-vis* its environment, but this applies in many instances to new comprehensives being built in areas where traditional, more selective forms prevailed. Certainly, the history of *political forces* surrounding the Countesthorpe case are unique to its setting but, seen from an international vantage point, they don't markedly differ from the experiences I have heard discussed by, for example, German educators trying to implement comprehensives in certain conservative areas of their country. There are some very interesting stories from Bavaria and Baden-Würtemburg that I believe would give the Countesthorpe staff heart. I am aware of similar pressures occurring in Sweden when the first comprehensives appeared. Even in America, with its long high school tradition, there are still political pressures growing out of feelings that the high school system forces social conformity, does not allow the gifted and uniquely able students to grow and forces feelings of failure on students who have trouble achieving academically. In Europe these fears translate through the political process into issues of maintenance of class structure and national tradition versus achieving social equality. These issues seemed, to the foreign observer, to be particularly dramatised in the Countesthorpe case as one read the *Leicester Mercury*'s early reports and heard parent and community concerns expressed relating to vandalism and the appearance of sloppy informality, lack of discipline and inadequate attention to cognitive growth. These are the fronts on which the comprehensive battle is frequently fought and the innovators involved often comment openly at IMTEC conferences about the constant struggle to maintain the essence of their innovations in the face of politically motivated pressures.

Another area in which Countesthorpe appears similar to other developments is in the rather recent interest in creating *alternative educational programmes* with a single system. Perhaps the most dramatic of these developments currently being watched by IMTEC is the Experimental Schools Program in America whose avowed aim was to create a wide variety of options in areas where there were vastly different ethnic and social groupings that demand different treatments from the public education system (in American terminology this means financed by taxation, not private fees). As a result of this programme cities like Minneapolis, Minnesota, now have whole groups of alternative schools ranging from 'free' schools to highly structured, traditional schools. Many of these options incorporate the 'community college' aspect developed at Countesthorpe, with heavy involvement of the community in both the educational programmes offered and the governance of the schools. Marshall High School and the Free School in Minneapolis would be interesting comparisons to Countesthorpe. In addition to this US model, there is much in the Countesthorpe case that is similar to the Oslo Forsøksgymnas, an alternative upper secondary school in Oslo run primarily by students. I know there has been a good deal of contact between this school and Countesthorpe over the years and, though I believe the Oslo school relies more heavily on student decision-making than Countesthorpe, there are remarkable similarities in the student–staff relationships, range of curricular choice and use of a consensus model of decision-making. There are no doubt many other examples (i.e. the 'minischools' in Denmark) with which I am relatively unfamiliar.

Organisationally Countesthorpe is similar to other large comprehensives in, among others, the following ways:

(a) most of the new comprehensives have developed new levels of participation in decision-making, particularly concerning students' involvement;

(b) as mentioned above, the new comprehensives are trying to involve the wider community in the school in new ways, including integrating adult education with the regular school programme and using community activities as part of the educational programme;

(c) with the new school forms, traditional dress requirements are typically relaxed, as are the relationships between students and teachers;

(d) following on (c), new relationships between the school leadership and staff are developing;

(e) increased emphasis on the pastoral function of the school is calling forth new organisational forms in which the teacher is recognised as an important counsellor as well as instructor;

(f) buildings tend to be open-spaced and carpeted with flexible interior design.

In addition to these features, it seems that most of these innovations create extreme fatigue in the initial leadership. I am familiar with Oslo Forsøksgymnas, a comprehensive school in Freiburg, Germany, and the Free School in Minneapolis, all of which underwent leadership change within two or three years of starting. The McMullen situation is not unique.

In curriculum matters, Countesthorpe seems similar to other schools in the following ways:

(a) the heavy reliance on self-instruction packages and multi-media approaches to instruction are common in secondary education, particularly in Sweden;

(b) most comprehensives have vastly expanded the options available to students, some of which are entirely new areas and some of which are combinations of old areas (i.e. integration of drama and music);

(c) the comprehensives I know all offer some form for students to qualify on standard college entrance exams, even in the most progressive ones;

(d) most comprehensive curricula offer a career or vocational option;

(e) the interpersonal relationships between student and teacher during the instruction process are becoming more organic, more two-way than in traditional programmes;

(f) many of the comprehensives in Europe are developing very strong international ties, not only through their language departments but also through their student exchange programmes and leadership training in institutions like IMTEC.

In summary, Countesthorpe fits in an overall trend in secondary education in which systems are seeking new ways of meeting both societal and individual student and staff needs. As new models develop, new answers to enigmatic questions emerge. However, the trend also shows that the needs of students and the needs of teachers interact and that the instruction process must be viewed organically.

WHAT MAKES COUNTESTHORPE UNIQUE?

Much has already been written in this book concerning the uniqueness of Countesthorpe. My purpose here is simply to make some subjective judgements about its uniqueness from an international perspective, judgements that grow out of conversations with educators from various countries who have engaged in analyses of the Countesthorpe case study at various IMTEC seminars.

Seen internationally, it is not so much what is being done at Countesthorpe that is unique (the forms of the organisation and educational process are not, in and of themselves, unique), but how it is being done, the depth to which basic innovative goals are pursued. In order to give some structure to the following, I have grouped innovative characteristics under three broad, and by no means exclusive, headings: those occurring internally in the school and its operation; those occurring at the interface between the school and its environment and those for which I could not find a ready category.

Internal features

The dominant unique feature internal to the school is, in my opinion and that of a majority of the IMTEC course participants, the decision-making structure. As mentioned above, many new comprehensives have more participatory forms of governance but none, to my knowledge, has gone as extensively into the moot form of governing with its extensive, documented 'common law' form for policy-making. Because Countesthorpe has stayed with this form even after the school grew, several obvious phenomena have occurred that set the school apart from its brothers and sisters in other lands:

(a) Despite bitter battles and great fatigue, important key staff members have stayed with the school, lending continuity through leadership changes and major growth periods.

(b) The governance form, established from the opening day of the school, gave the staff a chance to *own* the goal structure and, to this day, five years hence, there is remarkable adherence to the original objectives. Activities have changed as staff sought new and better ways to meet student needs, but the goals have remained and are referred to frequently by staff in almost religious ways. This kind of strong self-concept is unique for a new comprehensive.

(c) With the exception of the Oslo Forsøksgymnas, I cannot think of one new comprehensive in which the headmaster has given up so much decision-making power to the staff. This may have prolonged some decisions but it has provided excellent in-service training for the staff in group processes and school management.

(d) Many new organisations fail to build methods for conflict management and resolution. Countesthorpe, judging from copies of moot minutes on file at IMTEC, not only recognised the value of conflict but seems to have a method whereby it can be open, even to the public, and still result in productive decisions.

Another unique feature is the nature of role relationships in the school. Teachers and students are on a first-name basis and staff and students seem to mingle more than I've observed in other schools. A unique degree of tolerance seems to be engendered for relaxed behaviour in the school. This is, of course, consistent with the goal of creating a sense of security in students that is, in the view of Countesthorpe, essential for learning. With the advent of the teams, teachers took on much more of the adviser or pastoral role that very often is left to specialised personnel in large comprehensives. My conversations with the staff indicated that many of them felt this added role helped them directly in assisting students in setting individual goals in the group context of the teams. As a final observation on unique role relations at Countesthorpe, I have to note that it is rare that leadership changes are handled in rapidly changing situations with the smoothness and goal-consistency of the transfer from McMullen to Watts. The leader of Countesthorpe has only one vote in the moot and must continually earn his status. This is not the way most top school authority figures function.

Much has been written in this book about the curriculum at the school and, as mentioned, from an international perspective it is not unique in and of itself. However, educators can learn a great deal from the way it is created, the way it is constantly questioned by staff and students and how the two work synergistically in creating new, exciting materials. The resistance of the school to adopting programmes that involve heavy rote learning in order for students to pass certain standardised college entrance exams is another interesting example of the dogged adherence to the original goals of creating inquiring, creative minds.

School–environment interface
It is rare in my short international experience to see a new, controversial innovation start with the fanfare that seems to surround Countesthorpe. The school has been extremely visible from opening day, a visibility that has opened it to criticisms from the press and international educators that many others avoid merely because it is difficult to know what is going on. There are frequent visitations to the school by local and international educators; there are studies made, inspections, TV documentaries and deep scrutiny by the *Leicester Mercury*, all of which adds to the attention the school gets. I don't say this is good or bad; it is unique in my experience.

Unlike other alternative forms (i.e. the Experimental Schools Program in America and Oslo Forsøkgymnas) Countesthorpe has a fixed attendance area and, though students can choose to come to the school, the bulk of the students attend because they are in the attendance zone. This means that the school has a broadly mixed student body in terms of social background and the related differences in learning styles.

Another feature of the school–environment interface is, of course, the way in which the school has become the target of major political issues, not only in terms of the comprehensive issue mentioned above, but also in terms of the consolidation of the county and city systems in Leicestershire. Again it is unique that a single school becomes so deeply embroiled in these broader issues.

Other areas
Unlike many new schools that depart radically from normal procedure, Countesthorpe is not designated as an experimental school. I am aware of no ongoing staff evaluator function or any unusual accountability the school feels towards the central administration. It is funded as other upper secondary schools in Leicestershire and does not receive unusual resources in any way.

The final uniqueness of the school, seen internationally, is the fact that it began with a student body in the 11–14 range rather than the expected

14–18 range. To my knowledge, very few schools, planned as upper secondary schools, have to adjust their procedures as dramatically as Countesthorpe did. After three years of working with the lower age-group students, the lower secondary building was finished on the same campus and opened in the midst of political battles over leadership and style. (School uniforms were required in the lower school, for example.) This is a unique situation.

HOW CAN STUDIES BE PRODUCTIVELY USED IN THE FUTURE?

It might be useful to end with a few comments on how this book might be used in international training. For the continuing international interest in better understanding of the process of innovation in education, the Countesthorpe case presents many hypotheses and areas of study. It can be an important stimulus to research, particularly in the areas of leadership, governance, the political dimensions of educational change, the viability of various organisational forms for different types of innovation and, generally, how curriculum can be developed to meet the needs of youth.

In addition to research topics suggested from the work already done on Countesthorpe, the process by which a case study like this has evolved raises pedagogical possibilities for teaching about the change process in more effective ways. It is difficult to capture the *time dimension* of change in a single case study. The development of the Countesthorpe case from the Bernbaum study, through my updated work with 'learning packets' to the continuous dialogue about recent developments at the school, suggests a 'prediction–test–prediction' model for stimulating student inquiry.

Such a model would simply be based on providing students with 'baseline' data in the form of an initial case study. Based on this data, predictions can be made or strategy games played given certain assumptions. These predictions or strategies can then be compared to reality data from current developments. Too often contact between a case study and the real situation is lost. It is too easy to get lost in the biases of a single researcher and his or her predictions. The Countesthorpe case is becoming increasingly useful as a 'prediction–test–prediction' model.

Finally, the book can be an important testimony to the fact that innovation in education in general and finer distinctions of the management function in particular are, indeed, complex areas of study. It becomes part of an unfolding history that every educator contemplating or actually engaged in an innovation would do well to study. Frightening as many of the facets of Countesthorpe's history are, it can only give courage to those who are convinced that schools need not wait for society to define their every form and rule. Some schools can look beyond today to tomorrow's needs and muster the human perseverance and openness required to grow in this business.

23

Countesthorpe Revisited

A Personal View, May 1974

PETER CORNALL

PETER CORNALL was educated at Clifton and Balliol College, Oxford. His teaching life has been very much within the setting of the development of grammar and secondary modern schools into comprehensives. He was the first director of studies at Crown Woods School 1959–64, assistant education officer for Wiltshire, then the headmaster appointed to steer the amalgamation that became West Bridgford Comprehensive School, Nottingham. He is now headmaster of Carisbrooke School, Isle of Wight. After his third visit to Countesthorpe in May 1974 he wrote a report for study by his own staff. We are indebted to him for permission to publish it here.

At my third visit to Countesthorpe College I began to perceive – at least I think I did – a fundamental principle which informs all its singular responses to the problems of the senior comprehensive school. This principle is the avoidance of divisions from which conflict, open or concealed, could develop. This may be thought, with the advantage of hindsight, to be a natural extension of the reduction of barriers which true comprehensive education is intended to achieve.

In most schools there are two major relationships which can produce conflict : first, the division between teachers and conscript pupils; second, that between the head (and perhaps his immediate deputies) and the remainder of the teaching staff. (Where the line of this split comes will depend on the nature of the hierarchy in each particular school.) The intensity of conflict and its frequency is to some extent modified by the attitudes of the various parties towards each other, but in most schools there will be conflict, often open between staff and students, usually latent between the 'top brass' (significant phrase?) and the majority staff group. The typical demand that somehow the head should 'do something' about growing student indiscipline is the classic illustration of the two types of conflict situation interacting; the answer to difficulties has to be repression (staff/student division), and the execution of the policy in the responsibility of the executive (the rank-and-file/brass hat division).

The tradition established at Countesthorpe rejects the inevitability of both conclusions by making a revolutionary new approach to all the relationships involved. No privileges are claimed by virtue of age (staff older than students) or by virtue of higher salary (staff with special appointments paid more than others); the only differences in amenity – very few – are those which derive directly and unavoidably from difference in function. Not only are all teachers able to play a part in making appointments to the staff: the views of students are also sought and considered. There is no staff-room; staff and students share the same common areas. Smoking is allowed in two areas only and at two short periods in the day; if they wish to smoke, staff must there join those students who have permission to smoke. They do not smoke elsewhere. Regulations such as this are the result of discussions at year level leading to debate in the moot, a meeting of the whole community, which *everyone* may attend and at which *everyone* may vote. The use of first names in common between all members of the community – staff, students, clerical assistants, caretaking staff.

At Countesthorpe the avoidance of possible areas of staff/student conflict is carried farther than in most schools: there is no uniform; there is no wish to restrict the movement of students from the site at dinner-time; with the help of parents, a formula has been found to allow smoking to come into the open, under a measure of control, rather than remain 'underground'; most significant of all, there are no punishments. There is a parallel rejection of the hierarchical relationships which tend to produce tensions between head and staff. The influence of the principal depends on the respect which his views may earn in discussion rather than upon the authority with which he is invested by virtue of his appointment. Delegation of responsibility extends to areas such as the appointment of staff and the allocation of the College's allowances between the different spending groups. Both are dealt with by committees of the standing committee (see below). Above all, decisions about College policy are all taken either at the infrequent moots or at the weekly standing committee meetings, which all may attend and at which anyone may introduce an item; the standing committee itself consists of one quarter of the staff, serving for one quarter of the year, with principal and deputies *ex officio*. Among the staff, all of whom have joined the College because they wished to do so, there is a team relationship from which the attitude of 'them and us' seems almost to have been banished.

How is the conflict-avoiding principle worked out in the main function of a school – to provide education? Quite simply, a student is expected to work at certain core subjects – English, maths, social studies, religious education – and to choose additional subjects *if he or she wishes*. Because all the work of the school is based on very extensive use of individual learning methods, there is no need to require that each student chooses some fixed number of subjects : nor is it necessary that classes shall consist of students of comparable ability or similar age. A student's time may be divided among few such choices, or among rather more. Even within the core subjects, the methods used allow each student a considerable discretion, subject to the tutor's advice, over what his or her programme of work shall consist of. The compulsion to attend, and to study, is still present, even for the most reluctant – but many of the obligations, the requirement to choose between equally unpalatable alternatives, the compulsory physical education – so greatly disliked by some girls – all these are removed, and with them resentments with which most schools have to contend.

There is yet one more very important achievement at Countesthorpe – the total avoidance of the artificial split between pastoral and academic responsibility for students. Many of us have regarded it as unavoidable, and yet have still been conscious of a profound unreason in the appearance of separating each boy or girl into two, the person and the scholar, and we are accustomed to devote much effort into countering the effects of doing so. When new students enter Countesthorpe, they become members of a team which consists of about 170 students and six teacher-tutors; the tutors will include one or two teachers of English, a teacher of maths and a teacher of the humanities. Besides these, one or two staff from other curricular areas will have volunteered to join the team. These staff *are* the pastoral care system for the students in their area for the two years they are together. They will teach the students for whom they are responsible, and they will guide them in their choice of other work. If they are in trouble it will be dealt with inside the team; the tutor is the normal channel of communication between home and school both about work and conduct; he can always draw immediately on the team's knowledge of each student's work in core subjects, while he must turn to others for information about science, languages, etc. Court reports are produced by the team and passed to a deputy principal. If the principal or one of his deputies is approached direct, the team is invariably drawn in. Sex education is dealt with through the teams. Remedial needs are co-ordinated for the teams by one of the deputy principals. A team member may occasionally wish to *talk* over a problem with principal or Deputy, but he will rarely wish to *hand* it over, and see it go outside the team. When a staff vacancy occurs in a team, the advertisement is drawn up by the team, and the team has a decisive voice in the choice of a successor. The team decides how its separate allocation of money is to be spent. For both the staff and the students concerned, it is in the operations of the team that the democratic process is most obvious, though without formality.

The pattern of teaching at Countesthorpe is tremendously flexible, because the teachers have never accepted the one teacher/one room/one class formula. In another school, a decision that a student shall not take a subject, or shall drop a subject, immediately causes a problem – where shall he or she go? What shall be done instead, and with whom? At Countesthorpe, because of the dependence on individualised learning techniques, the time used for the remaining subjects can simply expand to take up the slack, but without causing the danger of idleness which in other schools would be feared when, for example, a student in the sixth was allowed to drop one A level subject halfway through the course.

The team situation can ease conflict in another way; and this applies both to teams working in the core subjects and to those in some of the other curricular areas; a teacher need never feel himself with no alternative to 'slogging it out' with a difficult student on his own in one teaching space. Dangerous confrontations can be side-stepped when it is easy to suggest a temporary move to some individual task with another colleague working within the team area. Such a transfer does not carry the punitive connotation which in many schools is present when a student is 'sent out of the room', because independent study is a *normal* part of every student's day. In any case, teachers feel less isolated, and the class–teacher challenge rarely presents itself in the type of teaching situations which involve several colleagues in associated spaces.

The sceptic may sensibly ask whether, besides conflict, *learning* is also being avoided. In the first place, some students will certainly not be studying as wide and as balanced a curriculum as some of us might wish. The answer would be, I think, that those who reject certain areas of the curriculum, after a thorough process of advice from tutors and others, would almost certainly have lacked the will to succeed in that area. At Countesthorpe, *physical presence without motivation is regarded as an evil to be avoided.* (The areas to which this rejection can apply are languages, sciences, technical studies, physical education and creative arts.) Secondly, just how much is learnt through the widespread use of individual learning methods? The school will claim modestly that the standards reached are at least as good as those elsewhere, and that the use of these techniques allows teachers to 'individualise' their teaching by permitting special aspects of subjects to be pursued with small groups and with individuals. This is the answer to the problem of how to ensure that the most able are taken forward at the proper pace, and of how to enrich the work programme by introducing topics with a limited but important appeal.

What has been done has only been possible because of the readiness of the teachers to work in mixed teams, rather than in English, maths, world studies team; by their readiness to give very considerable amounts of time and energy out of school hours to the meetings inherent in the whole system; by their acceptance of a life-style which many teachers would imagine must be distasteful. To an important degree, the special nature of the buildings has helped and encouraged the team approach and the individual learning – but I would not be willing to say that without special buildings these developments are out of the question. The adaptations which are most important take place, if they happen at all, *within the minds* of those involved. We have to remember that the Countesthorpe staff were recruited for the special objectives of the College. I fancy that if other teachers decided to accept the order of priorities established there, the purely physical problems would quickly seem secondary; not insignificant, not without severe handicapping effects, but secondary nonetheless.

Any attempt to estimate the extent of Countesthorpe's success is a presumption after so short a visit; one can record only impressions, and one can draw on previous knowledge of people. I *know* that the principal is a man for whom levels of attainment could *never* become unimportant, even set against the virtues of social harmony; his acceptance of the potential effectiveness of Countesthorpe's teaching/learning methods, whatever their development problems may be, is for me a guarantee that this school is not the 'holiday camp' which some of its students name it in affectionate mockery. I sensed the relative freedom from tension and conflict, which contrasts so markedly with the hateful daily problems of 'good order and discipline' which absorb so much nervous energy in many schools. There is a certain amount of litter in the grounds, which from time to time the whole community moves out to purge away from its environment. There *has been* damage – the product of the early months when an unprepared generation of students left its mark to deface what it had too little time to enjoy: but it was good to sense the strong confidence that when the evidence of this inevitably traumatic time has been removed there will be for fewer tensions to be worked out in this unpleasant way. [*A prediction that has been fulfilled. Ed.*]

I suggested at the beginning of this paper that the avoidance of divisions appeared to be the fundamental principle of the Countesthorpe philosophy, and that the attempt to minimise all conflict had been carried there to the farthest point so far seen within the state system of secondary education. The staff of this school have openly recognised a fact about secondary schools today which others have shrunk from admitting even to themselves – *that there are no longer any sanctions*: while it has long been obvious that 'management' possessed no coercive powers over teachers, it now has to be acknowledged that staff as a whole have no such powers over students. To an increasingly large number of teachers in senior secondary schools, corporal punishment becomes a daily more ludicrous answer to the problems of our time, while exclusion, beyond a brief cooling-off period, runs entirely counter to society's decision that schooling should be extended.

If there are no sanctions, at least in the terms we used to accept, upon what alternative must we depend for effective operation in our schools? The answer can only be this: *upon the effectiveness of our relationships,* within an appropriate framework. The young people cannot be coerced, nor are they generally in awe of us because we are older; indeed, sometimes the opposite reaction is all too obvious. Our strength lies elsewhere – in our patience; our capacity to absorb; our consistent firmness; our ability to encourage and to give obviously fair and useful advice; our appeal to good sense and to reason, to the rights of others and to a sense of obligation; if we have earned respect, we can appeal to a reluctance to forfeit our regard be rejecting our advice or persisting in conflict with us. In all of this, our maturity should be of the kind that consistently adheres to offering sincere help, and dislikes manipulation simply for the sake of social control, even though there will be times when this is necessary for the sake of others.

If I am right in what I am trying to say here, then it would be better for all of us if we stopped pretending that a punishment system is still an effective answer to our problems of control; if we recognised that such a system is inconsistent with the basic purposes of a school in the final years before full citizenship is achieved; if we faced up to replacing our hybrid systems with an *all-out* attempt to break down the 'them and us' attitudes which exacerbate so many of the 'generation gap' conflicts both inside schools and outside. Certainly this facing-up would be infinitely better than maintaining the myth, seemingly cherished by so many of the 'front line' teachers, that 'they' (head, deputies, year tutors, etc.) *could* deal with problem students if only they had the determination to do so, instead of inclining to a flabby tolerance. To believe in this myth is to be out of touch with the complex realities of a secondary school's relationships with society today – parents, councillors, officials, social workers, the press and other media, ratepayers, and most important of all its 'clients' themselves. Perhaps teachers who feel that they bear the brunt of facing difficult students must come to recognise that there is a strong parallelism between the security and near-invulnerability which they enjoy as professionals, *vis-à-vis* both senior colleagues and their employers, and the security of tenure which the coming of comprehensive education has given to students of compulsory school age. May it also be true that as students see and hear their teachers pursuing their professional objectives with greater trustfulness, they too will be encouraged to be assertive?

Countesthorpe is showing us an alternative direction in which to seek solutions; some may say that what it offers is no more than a different myth – of a Utopia where what is inconsistent with the myth is disregarded. Perhaps it is only by myths that human societies can be sustained, or rather can sustain themselves; even if this is the truth of the matter, the choice of which myth to adopt is still significant. If there are grounds for thinking that traditional attitudes will no longer serve, we must be grateful for those who have laboured to offer us a glimpse of what could take their place.

PART IX
TAILPIECE

24

Two Poems

JANICE CLARKE

JANICE CLARKE was a student at Countesthorpe for the whole of its first five years. Her stories and poems constantly returned to the theme of self-exploration. When she was a sixth former two subjects inspired some of her strongest poetry, both in free form and close verse. One was the response to drama in performance; the other was the relationship between experience and words. We conclude this book with two of Janice's poems, one on each of these themes. Since writing them Janice has left to take up studies as an undergraduate at Keele University.

Is my poetry part of me?
Are the words all of me,
Or is there another part
Which doesn't cry out to become words?
There are inactive moments
When nothing seems to grasp
Hold of my thoughts
And direct them towards darkness.
At other times my mind relishes
In deep, dark, searching questions,
And produces no answers,
But an abundance of despair.
It snatches at all that is useless
And takes it inside,
Partly digesting and taking in the misery
So that it becomes part of me.
Often, for days it drowns all else
Which could care to wander in.
Other moments do exist
In which peaceful thoughts
Soak into myself.
But black moments appear
More often and in greater quantity:
Yet these are moments of production.
They are creativity!

AFTER *KING LEAR*

Strip away the meaningless factory,
The confined office blocks,
The barren concrete streets
And find a real world.
Remove the manipulated, distorted reason,
And replace it with true feeling,
Which will come through
Not turning to knock others down,
But through experiencing that
Which you inflict upon others.
And find a more real self.
Individuals who have thought
Of what it means to live
And that it must be experienced
Before it seems fitting to die,
Before accepting there is nothing left.
I will never reach the understanding
That it is a relief to die.
Always there is another bend
In the path I am bound to follow,
Which hides perhaps greater horror
Or a more fulfilling need to go on.
I can never see beyond the bend
To discover where all will end.

Reading List

(titles marked * make direct reference to Countesthorpe)

*Armstrong, Michael, 'Reconstructing Knowledge: an example', *Forum for the Discussion of New Trends in Education*, Vol. 17, No. 2 (Spring 1975)

Bantock, G. H., *Education in an Industrial Society* (Faber, 1963)

Bantock, G. H., *Freedom and Authority in Education* (Faber, 1975)

Barnes, D., *From Communication to Curriculum* (Penguin, 1976)

Barnes, D., Britton, B. and Rosen, H., *Language, the Learner and the School* (revised edn, Penguin, 1971)

Berg, Leila, *Risinghill, Death of a Comprehensive School* (Penguin, 1968)

*Bernbaum, Gerald, 'Countesthorpe College' in *Case Studies of Educational Innovation: II, At the Regional Level* (OECD, 1972)

Chanan, G. and Gilchrist, L., *What Is School For?* (Methuen, 1974)

Dalin, Per, *Strategies for Innovation in Education* (Paris, OECD 1972)

*Daniels, D. J., ed., *New Movements in the Study and Teaching of Chemistry* (Maurice Temple Smith, 1975)

D'Arcy, Pat, *Reading for Meaning*, 2 vols (Hutchinson Education, 1973)

Freire, Paulo, *Pedagogy of the Oppressed* (Penguin, 1972)

*Green, Eric, ed., *Towards Independent Learning in Science* (Hart-Davis of Granada Publishing, 1975)

*Holly, Douglas, *Beyond Curriculum* (Hart-Davis MacGibbon, 1973; Palladin, 1974)

Holt, John, *How Children Fail* (Pitman Publishing Corporation, 1964; Penguin, 1969)

*Macbeath, John, ed., *A Question of Schooling* (Hodder & Stoughton, 1976)

*Mason, Stewart C., ed., *In Our Experience* (Longman, 1970)

Neill, A. S., *Summerhill* (Penguin, 1968)

*Pedley, Robin, *The Comprehensive School* (Penguin, 4th edn, 1969)

*Prescott, William, *Portrait of Countesthorpe College, Case Study* 5.E203 (The Open University, 1976)

*Rée, Harry, *Educator Extraordinary. The Life and Achievement of Henry Morris* (Longman, 1973)

*Riley, Ann and Stamatakis, Kathy, 'Countesthorpe College, an Observant Study', *Forum*, Vol. 16, No. 3 (1974)

Simon, Brian, *The Common Secondary School* (Lawrence & Wishart, 1955)

Simon, Brian, *Studies in the History of Education*, 3 vols (Lawrence & Wishart, 1960, 1965, 1974)

*Simon, B and Benn, Caroline, *Half Way There* (Penguin, 2nd edn, 1972)

*Taylor, Philip and Walton, Jack, eds, *The Curriculum Research, Innovation and Change* (Ward Lock Educational, 1973)

*Turner, Barry, ed., *Discipline in Schools* (Ward Lock Educational, 1973)

*Watts, John, *Teaching* (David & Charles, 1974)

Writing Across the Curriculum 11–16 Years, Schools Council and London University Institute of Education Joint Project, Pamphlet series including *Keeping Options Open* and *Writing in Science* (published by the project, ULIE, 1974)

Index